REAGANOMICS
Rhetoric vs. Reality

D1216921

REAGANOMICS
Rhetoric vs. Reality

Frank Ackerman

South End Press   **Boston**

First printing
Library of Congress Number: 82-80689
ISBN paper: 0-89608-141-9
ISBN cloth: 0-89608-142-7

Cover design by Kathy Moore
Produced by the South End Press collective

South End Press
302 Columbus Ave.
Boston, MA 02116

Table of Contents

ABOUT THE AUTHOR

Frank Ackerman received his Ph.D. in economics from Harvard University. He has been an editor of *Dollars and Sense* since 1974 and has also contributed articles to the *National Catholic Reporter, Colliers Encyclopedia, The Nation, Monthly Review, Socialist Review, Radical America* and the *Review of Radical Political Economics*. He is married, has one daughter and lives in Somerville, Massachusetts.

Acknowledgments

A number of people helped make this book possible. Arthur MacEwan, Jim Campen and Kathy Moore read the entire manuscript as I produced it, and offered valuable suggestions throughout. Arthur and Jim are also the authors of a critique of supply-side economics which is the basis for a large chunk of Chapter 3. Kathy also designed the cover of the book. Mark Breibart, Frank Broadhead, Faye Brown, Dick Cluster, Jean Kluver and Dan Luria contributed useful comments on various chapters and steered me to important sources of information. John Schall of South End Press originally talked me into writing this book, and guided me cheerfully and rapidly through the editorial process.

Portions of Chapter 2 first appeared in a different form in my review of *Free to Choose,* which was published in the *National Catholic Reporter* and in *Dollars & Sense.* An early draft of Chapter 4 was condensed and adapted into a two-part series in *Dollars & Sense,* in February and March, 1982. New material has been added since that version, and one serious error has been corrected—the account of the CIA's estimates of Soviet military spending was confused in the *D&S* version, and has been finally straightened out with the help of Franklyn Holzman, the leading liberal critic of the CIA statistics.

My acknowledgments would not be complete without mentioning David Stockman. Although we have never met, I have often felt that he and I are quite similar. We are about the same age, we were both active in the movement against the Vietnam war while in college, we are both interested in the U.S. economy today. How charming to discover, midway through writing this book, that we also share the same doubts about the honesty, the justice and the effectiveness of the policies he is working so hard to implement! Quotes from his true confessions in the December 1981 *Atlantic Monthly* naturally appear throughout the book.

Finally, I owe a collective word of thanks to the past and present members of *Dollars & Sense.* I have been on the staff of the magazine for eight years, taking part in an exciting group process of research and writing about the U.S. economy.

I have borrowed sentences and paragraphs from *D&S* articles here and there in the following pages; in many cases I remember all too well how hard we worked on writing clear explanations of complex economic issues, and I see no way to do any better. If you like this book, you can get monthly coverage of the economy from a very similar point of view by subscribing to *Dollars & Sense*, 38 Union Square, Room 14, Somerville, MA 02143. The price, in 1982, is $12 a year.

INTRODUCTION

Do You Believe in Magic?

The program we have developed will break (the) cycle of negative expectations. It will revitalize economic growth, renew optimism and confidence, and rekindle the Nation's entrepeneurial instincts and creativity.

The benefits to the average American will be striking. Inflation—which is now at double digit rates—will be cut in half by 1986. The American economy will produce. . . . nearly 3 million more (jobs) than if the status quo in government policy were to prevail. The economy itself should break out of its anemic growth patterns to a much more robust growth trend of 4 to 5 percent a year. These positive results will be accomplished simultaneously with reducing tax burdens, increasing private saving, and raising the living standard of the American family.

—The White House, *A Program for Economic Recovery*, February 1981.

If Ronald Reagan's economic program could live up to its press releases, it would be magical indeed. Yet to date the country appears less than enchanted by Reaganomics. Two rather different spells have been cast, both failing to produce what most of us would call success. The first, the big tax cut, was the star of the 1980 election campaign. According to the doctrines of "supply-side economics" (see Chapters 2 and 3), lower tax rates would do the trick alone, stimulating such a surge in incomes that tax revenues would not fall. No budget cuts were necessary, save for attacks on waste and fraud.

Soon after being elected, the incoming administration proclaimed its discovery that an "economic Dunkirk" loomed on the horizon. Spiralling inflation and budget deficits were so serious a threat that tax cuts alone would not suffice. Tight monetary policies (high interest rates and limits on funds available for borrowing) and moves toward a balanced budget were also vital. In other words, old-fashioned conservative economics with its built-in tendency toward recessions—an unpopular approach which would not have helped Reagan on the campaign trail—was quickly reintroduced just in case the supply-siders turned out to be a teensy bit overoptimistic.

This book is an explanation and a critique of Reaganomics. It is based on a decidedly unmagical view of the economy, and of the failings of both old and new styles of conservative policy. In brief, the argument is as follows.

On the list of reasons for Ronald Reagan's triumph in 1980, the economic mess of the 1970s probably stands at the top. This mess was no mere reflection of the intellectual or personal weaknesses of Reagan's predecessors. It represented a long-term crisis of our economic system. Chapter 1 analyzes that crisis. The United States enjoyed economic growth with little inflation for most of the 1950s and 1960s due to uniquely favorable, temporary circumstances. Changes in those circumstances in the late '60s and early '70s led to the slower growth, higher unemployment and faster inflation of the last ten years. Reaganomics rests on a shallow view of the crisis of the 1970s, one which scapegoats and misrepresents the complex role of government in the economy; and it offers only solutions that look worse than the problems did.

Conservative solutions to the economic crisis require reductions in most people's standards of living. Paradoxically, these solutions have become quite popular, coasting to an overwhelming victory in 1980. What political myths persuaded so many of us that less is more? Chapter 2 reviews recent bestsellers by leading ideologues of the old and new schools of conservative economics: *Free to Choose,* by Milton and Rose Friedman, and *Wealth and Poverty,* by George Gilder. The two books share certain fundamentals—the celebration of inequality, individual greed, and unleashed private enterprise, for instance. But they have their differences as well: the Friedmans exaggerate your power as a consumer, while Gilder exaggerates your chance of becoming a powerful businessman; the Friedmans believe in the old-time religion of fighting inflation with recession, while Gilder professes the new faith in supply-side miracles.

The big tax cut has always been the centerpiece of Reaganomics, the foundation of its popular support. Chapter 3 explains why the particular tax cut we got in 1981 is worth so little to most of us, and so much to those at the top. The Reagan tax cut is not only full of hidden biases; it is also unlikely to produce any noticeable "supply-side" effects on the economy. Supply-side theory claims that the tax cut will stimulate more work, more savings, and more investment—but both economic research and common sense argue against it.

Despite the widespread pressure to cut, one major area of government has been declared off limits to the budget-slashers, and endowed with rising appropriations instead. Chapter 4 examines the military and economic arguments surrounding the Pentagon budget boom. Military reality shows that the Soviet Union is not ahead of us by most important measures, and does not have the capacity to threaten a surprise "first strike" attack that would cripple our defenses. Moreover, many of our most expensive high-technology weapons are of no practical military use. As much as half of the military budget may be irrelevant to the defense of the United States and our allies in any conceivable conflict. Why, then, do we spend so much money? The answers include: preparing for offensive threats against weaker Third World nations; making work for people

and factories that would otherwise be idle; and creating a pa-
triotic-sounding excuse for cutting social welfare programs that
conservatives have always disliked.]

The Pentagon's billions aside, budget-cutting has become
quite fashionable in Washington. Chapter 5 focuses on the
Reagan cuts, both the ones achieved in the 1982 budget and
those proposed for 1983 and beyond. Most of the cuts come
out of a handful of programs benefitting the poor and the
jobless. There is a method to this meanness: deprived of government benefits, workers will be forced to beg for jobs, to
work for less than before. Income will trickle upward, from
employees' paychecks to employers' profits. The rhetoric of
the new federalism, of block grants, of turning over authority
to the states and cities, only conceals the reality that social
programs are being slashed—and slashed by decisions made
in Washington, not your state capitol or city hall. The ultimate
attack, on Social Security, may be waiting for us just beyond
the 1982 elections; like the other cuts, it is lacking in genuine
justification.

It is not only the people at the bottom of the working
population, those already dependent on governments benefits,
who are suffering from Reaganomics. The unions, too, are
under attack. Chaper 6 surveys the problems faced by the labor
movement on several fronts. Traditionally strong industrial
unions are on the defensive as a result of the continuing economic crisis; for them, the Reagan program consists of not
lifting a finger as entire industries and cities decline. Public
employee unions have been the other area of strength in the
labor movement of late; for them, Reaganomics offers budget
cuts, declining government employment, and the example of
the fate of the air traffic controllers as a warning to toe the
line. In occupational health and safety, a growing area of concern to many unions, Reagan's team has stopped progress dead
in its tracks.

The allegedly crushing burden placed on business by government regulation is a constant theme of conservatives. Chapter 7 explores the meaning of the crusade for deregulation.
Several different kinds of evidence show that the costs of regulation are routinely exaggerated, and the benefits understated
or ignored. Some regulations even force business to make

greater profits in spite of itself. Important industries do have reasons for their complaints: the auto companies would find it cheaper to produce more dangerous, polluting cars; the energy industry would like to strip-mine the West, drill offshore, and create potentially disastrous levels of air pollution in pursuit of its favored form of "energy independence." From the point of view of society as a whole, however, the benefits of many challenged regulations far outweigh the costs. Regulations may be under attack, not because of their failure, but because the very fact of their success in defending the interests of society against business is such a threat to Reagan's free-marketeers.

Finally, Chapter 8 suggests the outlines of an alternative to Reaganomics. That alternative requires restructuring the economy in a way that addresses the root causes of stagflation. This includes:

- A massive transfer of resources from the military to civilian needs, and reimposition of taxes on corporations and the rich;
- Civilian reindustrialization, moving labor and capital into conservation and clean energy development, mass transit and urban reconstruction;
- Maintenance of social services, including reform of Social Security financing, socialized medicine, and full employment and job retraining programs; and
- Price controls, backed up (as they were in World War II) by the government's willingness to engage in production of necessary goods and services when private enterprise refuses to.

This road begins to lead far from the familiar contours of the U.S. economy, but it is the only route to a society that works for most of us.

Soup Kitchens

CHAPTER 1

The Way the World Doesn't Work

How is it possible to raise defense spending, cut income taxes, and balance the budget, all at the same time? . . . "We've got to figure out a way to make (that question) fit into a plausible policy path over the next three years," Stockman said. "Actually, it isn't all that hard to do. . . ."

"The whole thing is premised on faith," Stockman explained. "On a belief about how the world works. The inflation premium melts away like the morning mist. It could be cut in half in a very short period of time if the policy is credible. That sets off adjustments and changes in perception that cascade through the economy. You have a bull market in '81, after April, of historic proportions."

—William Greider, "The Education of David Stockman," *Atlantic Monthly*, December 1981.[1]

At the time of the 1980 election, very few people understood Ronald Reagan's strange new belief about how the econ-

1

omy works. But everyone could see that the familiar old economic beliefs had failed miserably in the 1970s. Ask yourself whether you are better or worse off than you were four years ago, said candidate Reagan. It was the most memorable and most successful question of the campaign. Millions of people answered when they voted, not so much for the new as against the old.

The fact that many of us were becoming worse off was itself a sign of changing times. In the "good old days," a period including most of the 1950s and 1960s, wages climbed at a fairly steady pace. Inflation was all but unknown, and spells of high unemployment were brief.

Such times are long gone. By late 1981 the average worker's take-home pay bought less than it did in 1960, 16% below the record high level achieved in 1972. Family incomes, on average, roughly kept pace with inflation over the last ten years, but only because more and more families added second or third wage-earners. Levels of inflation, interest rates and unemployment that would have been called catastrophic a few years ago are now commonplace. In the 1970s, Republican and Democratic administrations alike seemed powerless to reverse our declining fortunes.

The new administration set out to change all that. Within a month of taking office Reagan announced his four-part "Program for Economic Recovery": civilian budget cuts and military buildup; tax cuts; rollback of federal regulations; and monetary policies that meant high interest rates. The first stages of this program were adopted with astonishing speed, much to the delight of some people. Generals and military contractors rejoiced at the shift of funds from civilian agencies to the Pentagon. Upper-income taxpayers enjoyed the particular biases of the Reagan tax cut. Corporate polluters breathed more freely thanks to deregulation.

Others were less satisfied. In the six months following the passage of the "Economic Recovery Tax Act of 1981" (as it was officially named), the ranks of the unemployed swelled by more than two million. Production and investment, as well as employment, headed down under the initial onslaught of Reaganomics. As Budget Director David Stockman soon learned, inflation did not melt away like the morning mist; the stock market rally expected "after April, of historic proportions," failed to materialize throughout 1981. By the middle of that year Stockman had concluded, "There was a certain dimension of our theory that was unrealistic. . . ."

That unrealistic dimension includes the entire analysis of what went wrong in the 1970s. The fundamental belief of the Reagan team is that private enterprise will work wonders as soon as the government leaves it alone. If the problem is government interference, the solution is to cut back everything (well, almost everything) the government does. Perhaps if the Reaganites were right about the problem, they would be right about the solution. But the world doesn't work that way.

Although the expanding role of government is of course involved in the economic problems which emerged in the 1970s, that is far from the whole story. A look at the real causes of our prolonged crisis will reveal the reasons why Reaganomics is no solution at all for almost all of us.

The economic problems of recent years are best understood by contrast with the less troubled era just after World War II. The growth and prosperity of much of the 1950s and 1960s rested on four favorable conditions: U.S. international power; abundant supplies of cheap oil; the growth of the auto/highway/suburb complex; and the particular nature of government intervention in the economy. Changes in all four areas in the late 1960s and early 1970s led to the "stagflation"— slow growth, unemployment and inflation—of the last decade. Traditional economic policies clearly failed to cope with these underlying problems in the 1970s. Reaganomics offers only a very partial, biased response to the causes of stagflation, and will provide, at best, a very partial, biased cure.

Once Upon a Time

The map of the route to crisis can begin at a point of undisputed success. We came out on top in World War II, economically as well as militarily. As the only major industrial nation to escape wartime destruction, the United States was in a position of unchallenged worldwide power after 1945. This was the first of the conditions allowing the decades of postwar prosperity.

The products of U.S. factories and farms were in demand around the world, leading to a steady trade surplus (that is, our exports were greater than our imports) through the mid-

1960s. U.S. foreign aid programs strengthened our trading partners, allowing them to buy more from us. For instance, the Marshall Plan helped revive wartorn European economies and reintegrate them with ours. As well as being our top export market, Europe soon became the fastest-growing area of foreign investment by U.S. corporations, returning an ever-growing stream of profits to this country.[2]

There were other places besides Europe where U.S. power was newly asserted. Our government moved rapidly to replace British and French influence in many Third World countries. Networks of aid, anti-communist alliances and military bases circled the globe. In the extreme we resorted to direct interventions: CIA-sponsored coups in Iran in 1953 and Guatemala in 1954, landings of the Marines in Lebanon in 1958 and the Dominican Republic in 1965, and the unsuccessful Bay of Pigs invasion of Cuba in 1962, to name the most blatant cases. Our increasingly multinational corporations followed the flag overseas, gaining access to Third World markets, low-wage labor, and cheap raw materials. Again, a rising tide of profits flowed homeward as U.S. business expanded abroad.

A massive military apparatus was created to defend this informal empire against real or imagined threats—often against nationalist movements in the more impoverished provinces of the "Free World" itself. And in the Cold War climate of the 1950s, few questions were asked about the need for military spending. After the Korean War, both direct military employment and weapons production remained higher than ever before in peacetime, boosting the rate of economic growth.

New industries sprang up as spin-offs from the military. Civilian aircraft and airlines were made possible by Air Force activity in developing planes and training pilots. Pentagon demand for small, lightweight, sophisticated electronics components helped launch the consumer electronics and computer industries. Nuclear energy, which at the time looked like a promising new technology for the future, was a byproduct of the nuclear weapons program. Not only U.S. international power, but also the arsenal which supported it, seemed to be good for business.

Among the treasures that multinational corporations brought back from their foreign adventures, none was more important than petroleum. The years after World War II were the years of cheap oil, from both foreign and domestic sources—the second of the conditions on which U.S. prosperity was based. New oil fields in Venezuela, Texas and the Middle East, almost all under American control, flooded the industrial world, driving out fuels such as coal and reshaping manufacturing and transportation.

Entire industries owe their existence, or their dominant technologies, to the former availability of cheap oil. As long as the price of petroleum was low, it made good business sense to use it extravagantly (by today's standards), to replace other materials and fuels with it. Thus petrochemical industries such as plastics and synthetic fibers used petroleum as their basic raw material. Agribusiness reorganized the farm with oil-powered machinery and oil-based fertilizers and pesticides. The rise of energy-guzzling air transportation, and the decline of energy-efficient railroads, could only have happened in a society that had liquid fuel to burn.

Cheap oil also made it possible for our lives to be transformed by the boom in automobiles, highways, suburbs and a host of related industries—the third condition underlying postwar prosperity. At the end of World War II there were 26 million cars on the roads, less than one for every five people; by 1973 there were 102 million, or one for every two people.[3] The creation of interstate highways and urban expressways allowed the ever-widening sprawl of suburbs and shopping centers, and the accompanying growth in construction and consumer goods. The value of new construction, corrected for inflation, grew by 4.3% per year from 1947 to 1965.[4] Factories as well as people moved to new suburban locations, as trucks replaced railroads in freight transportation. The strong unions of the day—the building trades, the teamsters, the auto, rubber and steel workers—were those whose members made and moved the products required for the suburban transformation.

The mystique of the marketplace, of business yearning to grow as soon as government gets out of the way, has become newly popular in the Reagan years. Contrary to this view, active government "interference" was one of the major conditions stimulating the post-World War II expansion. Federal government spending, a mere 3% of gross national product

(GNP) in 1929, never fell below 14% after 1945. Income taxes, previously paid only by the rich, were extended to almost everyone during World War II; after the war the broadened tax, and the expanded government role which it made possible, both survived. State and local government spending rose as well, and total government spending at all levels averaged 27% of GNP in the 1950s and early 1960s.[5]

With memories of the depression of the 1930s still relatively fresh, the belief became widespread that the government could and should step in to prevent recessions—or to speed up recovery when recessions did occur. The brief downturns of the era have been described as "hiccups between linked booms"; prompt increases in government spending helped ensure that they became nothing worse.

Moreover, the government spending of the early postwar years was heavily concentrated in programs that were attractive to business. In 1955, the military accounted for 32% of *all* public spending, federal, state and local; highways took 6%, and construction contracts for schools and other public buildings absorbed another several percentage points.

From the corporate point of view, military spending is the ideal government activity. In addition to whatever protection of foreign trade and investment it may provide, the Pentagon does not interfere with private industry. On the contrary, it offers lucrative contracts to aerospace and other firms, and at times stimulates the creation of spin-off industries as well. Similar advantages are provided by most government construction projects—juicy contracts, usually no competition with private business, and (as with highways) the creation of the basis for other industries to prosper.

The height of optimism about the government's ability to manage the economy was reached by the liberal advisors to the Kennedy and Johnson administrations in the 1960s. Presiding over the last long stretch of postwar prosperity, and over a rapid expansion in the size and role of the public sector, they claimed that they could "fine-tune" the economy to a desired level of employment and growth. But the grounds for their optimism, never terribly secure to begin with, were rapidly crumbling by the time they left office.

How the End Began

An impressive constellation of circumstances powered the postwar boom. But none of them were eternal. Many were unavoidably eroded by the very fact of twenty years of prosperity. In each of the four areas just described, changes appeared in the late 1960s and early 1970s. It is these changing conditions which caused the economic problems of recent years—and it is these changing conditions which Reaganomics does such a poor job of addressing.

Internationally, the wartime destruction of Europe and Japan was clearly temporary. U.S. trade and investment only hastened their return to the status of serious competitors. And with lower wages, newer plants and leaner management styles, they were serious competitors indeed. Suddenly, it seemed, the United States was no longer the only source of manufactured goods in the world. The U.S. trade surplus peaked in 1964 and then fell to a deficit, the first in the twentieth century, by 1971. The balance of trade has continued to worsen in most of the years since then; our trade deficit with Japan alone has often exceeded a billion dollars a month. The vanishing trade surplus has meant fewer jobs making products for export, and slower growth of the U.S. economy.

At about the same time, U.S. power in the Third World was meeting with decisive military defeat in Vietnam. In the wake of that war, liberation movements also came to power in Angola, Mozambique, Guinea-Bissau, Zimbabwe and Nicaragua. Each of these would, in an earlier time, have been met by the Marines. But in the 1970s defeat on the battlefield and domestic opposition to such wars foreclosed the option of intervention. Gloomy noises about the tides of world history were heard for a time in Washington and Wall Street.

It is not so coincidental that the end of cheap oil came in this same period. Back in the old days, the U.S. did not permit such impudence. In 1953 the nationalist government of Iran, which had seized control of that country's oil, was overthrown by the CIA. By 1973, though, when the first big price hike by OPEC (the Organization of Petroleum Exporting Countries) occurred, another U.S. military intervention was politically impossible. The rise of OPEC may be counted among the indirect effects of the war in Vietnam.

There was more to OPEC's triumph than just the anti-interventionist climate of the times. The world oil market was also quite favorable to the producing nations. In 1970 both U.S. and Venezuelan oil output had peaked and begun to decline, leaving consumers increasingly reliant on a handful of Middle Eastern countries. Then a brief worldwide economic boom in 1972–73 sent prices of other raw materials soaring. OPEC oil ministers undoubtedly noticed these trends, and seized on the first plausible excuse, the Middle East war in late 1973, to quadruple the price of their oil. But even with such a favorable market position, it is unlikely that OPEC would have tried anything so bold in the days when U.S. "gunboat diplomacy" reigned supreme.

The energy price explosion of the 1970s flattened oil-intensive industries. Since oil has become expensive, major airlines have frequently been on the brink of bankruptcy, agribusiness has been financially troubled and petrochemicals no longer look like the growth sector they once were. The oil companies, getting a cut of the new high prices, have continued to prosper; their customers have not. The massive U.S. investment in oil-hungry industries made economic sense only at pre-crisis prices. At today's energy prices it is unlikely that the present levels of replacing natural materials with plastics and synthetics, or ground transportation with airlines, or even railroads with cars and trucks, would ever have developed.

Growth based on autos, highways and suburbs had built-in limits, which were being felt even before the oil crisis. When all major cities are tied to one another with ribbons of concrete and ringed with suburbs and shopping malls, when every garage contains a car and many hold two, there is simply no room for more. Shifting patterns of population and industry may mean that construction continues, for instance, around some Sunbelt cities or "high-tech" enclaves. But overall the pace is necessarily far below the heyday of highways and suburbanization. The value of new construction, corrected for inflation, grew by an average of 0.5% a year from 1965 to 1978, far below its earlier pace (and after 1978 the bottom fell out of the construction business entirely). High gasoline prices make the most remote suburbs and longest commutes even less attractive than before, dampening the outer reaches of suburban sprawl. Also, just as the former strength of the building trades and industrial unions was based on the growth in autos, highways and suburbs, the present weakness of these unions can be traced to the long-term slump in their industries.

Finally, the nature of government intervention in the economy was also changing. For a while after World War II, most spending by the federal government was justified in Cold War terms. The interstate highways were supposed to facilitate rapid movement of troops and material in case of invasion. Even the school lunch program was said to boost military preparedness, since so many potential soldiers had flunked their physicals due to nutritional deficiencies in World War II.

But as the Russians persisted year after year in their stubborn refusal to invade Western Europe, Cold War politics gradually receded. The Pentagon's budget, though massive, barely kept up with inflation from 1955 to 1980 (the few peak years of Vietnam spending of course excepted). Other programs were expanding much faster. The two leading growth areas in public spending were retirement benefits and education; a host of smaller health and welfare programs were being created or expanded as well.

The growth of social programs has a contradictory effect on business. On the one hand, companies are happy to have a healthier, better educated workforce, to have the government pass out unemployment checks so that experienced workers stick around instead of leaving town during layoffs, and to have Social Security reduce the demand for private pensions.

On the other hand, this is an area where businessmen definitely find it possible to have too much of a good thing. In the 1960s and early 1970s the civil rights, anti-poverty and other movements forced the rapid increase of government benefits and services; at the same time the elderly, a quieter but fairly well-organized voting bloc, won Medicare and big boosts in Social Security payments. The sheer size of social welfare spending, the momentum of growth and the grassroots political initiative involved came to threaten corporate stability. Any income that people receive without working reduces their dependence on employers, and the trend seemed to be toward more and more non-wage income being made available to the poor. Budget cuts were almost impossible since benefits came to be viewed, and often legally defined, as rights to which people were entitled.

Under the impact of these changes, government spending rose more rapidly in the 1960s than before. The combined total of federal, state and local budgets reached 32% of GNP in the 1970s. (It did not, however, continue to rise beyond that; total public spending was not a significantly higher fraction of GNP in the second half of the 1970s than in the first.)[6]

The point is not that a magic number had been crossed, that government spending of 27% of GNP had been okay, but 32% somehow broke the bank. Indeed, private enterprise manages to thrive in Western European nations where public spending is routinely well above 32% of GNP. Rather, the problem was that the surge in spending was accompanied by the continuing shift into areas that business found less profitable and less controllable. The strength of anti-war sentiment held down both the size and the duration of military spending in Vietnam, and then put the lid back on the Pentagon budget for the 1970s—allowing social programs to grow again. By 1978 the military accounted for only 14% of all government spending and highways only 3%.

In short, government spending was shifting in a direction which was more helpful to many people, but less advantageous to business. At about the same time, U.S. international power was waning, energy was becoming expensive and the suburban boom was stalling. These are the changes that account for the stagflation of the 1970s, for the failure of traditional economic policy in that decade and for the likely failure of Ronald Reagan's programs as well.

The Stagnant Seventies

Before turning to Reagan's program it will be helpful to glance back at the failures of his predecessors. The particular obstacles on which their policies ran aground did not vanish when Reagan was elected.

Even in the earlier era of growth, the progress of the economy was never perfectly smooth. There were ups and downs in production and employment, though relatively more ups and fewer downs than in recent years. The claim that the economy could be "fine-tuned" to a desired level of employment has never been borne out in reality. Still, at least crude tuning of the volume of economic activity did seem to be within the government's reach.

Conventional economic policy relied heavily on the theory of the trade-off between inflation and unemployment. When more people are out of work, wages and prices are supposed to rise more slowly; with progress toward full employment, wages and prices are said to shoot up more rapidly. A graph of this relationship is enshrined in the literature of economics as the "Philips curve."

The trade-off theory is based on changes in the bargaining strength of capital and labor. When unemployment is very low, employed workers are secure in the knowledge that they are hard to replace; their bargaining position relative to their employers is strong and they are often able to win large wage gains and other concessions. Businesses pass on most or all of these increased labor costs in the form of higher prices. When unemployment is high, employed workers are easy to replace, their bargaining position is weak and large gains by labor are rare. Businesses have lower cost increases to pass on. And with consumer incomes down due to unemployment, it's not a great time for raising prices anyway. Thus prosperity causes inflation, and recession stops it. Garbed in varying jargons, this idea has been the basis of Republican and Democratic policy alike for decades.

The goal of economic policy, then, was to find and maintain the perfect amount of unemployment. Too much unemployment was clearly undesirable, and too little would provoke inflation. Two principal sets of tools were used in this effort: fiscal and monetary policy.

Fiscal policy means changing the levels of government spending and taxes. Raising government spending or cutting taxes—in other words, increasing the deficit—tends to put unemployed people back to work. For instance, suppose the government decides to build more missiles, or to cut taxes for the rich, who promptly buy more yachts. Then more people are hired to build missiles or yachts. Those workers buy more food and clothing, other workers are hired in the food and clothing industries, and so on. Conversely, cutting the budget or raising taxes—decreasing the deficit—tends to have the opposite effect, throwing people out of work.

Monetary policy means manipulating the rate of interest and the availability of money for loans. It is carried out through a series of arcane mechanisms controlled by the Federal Reserve System, the semi-autonomous federal agency which governs the nation's money and banking. A "tight money" policy means loans are expensive and hard to get, discouraging consumer borrowing to buy homes and cars, and business borrowing for expansion. The result is a drop in employment. "Easy money," a policy of low interest rates and easy access to loans, encourages debt-financed spending and helps put unemployed people back to work.

The dismal economic record of recent years has led many people to conclude that the theory of the trade-off between inflation and unemployment is no longer valid. After all, we seem to be enjoying the worst of both. Yet at any one time unemployment does slow inflation. The 1975 recession, in which the official unemployment rate briefly topped 9%, brought the rate of inflation down from 12.2% in 1974 to 4.8% in 1976.[7] Reagan's 1981–82 recession seems to be doing a similar job. Even oil prices roughly follow the theoretical pattern. The two big OPEC price hikes, in 1973–74 and 1979, were blamed on specific events in Middle Eastern politics, but happened to come at times when Western economies and oil imports had been growing for several years. In the recessions of 1975 and 1981–82 oil prices rose much more slowly, or even fell at times.

But if the inflation-unemployment trade-off still works at any one time, it appears to work worse and worse as time goes on. More and more unemployment is needed to achieve the same reduction in inflation. The situation may be compared to pumping the water out of an increasingly leaky boat. On any day the pump still works, but every day it takes more pumping to achieve the same reduction in wetness. In the language of economists, the terms of the trade-off between pumping effort and wetness, between unemployment and inflation, are worsening.

The changes in the four major bases of postwar prosperity, as discussed above, are in several ways responsible for the worsening terms of the trade-off between inflation and unemployment. Some of the effects are obvious. The oil crisis, for instance, has meant that any given level of unemployment is now accompanied by faster inflation than it would have been before 1973. Some of the effects are subtler ones, reshaping the struggle between labor and capital over wages and prices.

The very fact of stagnation, the slowing of economic growth, itself causes an increase in inflation. In the traditional metaphor, when the pie is growing, everyone can have a bigger slice with little conflict. But when the pie stops growing, any increase must come at someone else's expense. The "size of the pie," measured by GNP per worker (corrected for inflation), grew by an annual average of 2.6% from 1947 to 1966, but only 0.9% from 1966 to 1980. In the years of faster growth, both labor and capital came to expect that they could win steadily rising incomes; when growth began to sputter, the continuing demands for higher wages and profits came into conflict, adding to inflationary pressures. Consumer prices climbed by an annual average of only 2% from 1947 to 1966, compared to 8% from 1966 to 1980. The inflationary spiral was begun by deficit financing of the Vietnam war in the late 1960s, but continued well after war spending declined, in part due to the clashing expectations of labor and capital.

It was not only the memories of growth in past years that created expectations of rising wages and prices.The changing economic role of the government, in particular, reinforced that expectation. The growing public expenditure on programs such as unemployment compensation, food stamps and welfare made it possible for people to accept brief layoffs rather than taking any job, no matter how poorly paid. More broadly, the government's evident commitment to preventing major depressions encouraged workers and employers to resist wage and price cuts in recessions. If the return of prosperity is known to be right around the corner, a temporary drop in employment or sales has little effect on wages and prices. The more often that recessions turn out to be nothing serious, the less effective they become in scaring people.

The situation was quite different in the nineteenth century, when such amenities as unemployment benefits and government spending to promote full employment were virtually unknown. Superficially it was a century of success in controlling inflation: prices were lower in 1900 than in 1800. Nineteenth-century prices rose rapidly, especially during wars, but fell again during the frequent panics and depressions. In an old-fashioned depression, the trade-off was ruthlessly effective. Fear of starvation forced workers to bid their wages lower and lower, and the collapse of consumer markets forced companies to slash their prices. Few people would stand up in public and advocate this method of price control today. But it should not be forgotten that it is the principal method that has worked in the past.

Although the inflation-unemployment trade-off was steadily worsening in the 1970s, the old economic policies still worked after a fashion. Throughout the decade the Nixon, Ford and Carter administrations periodically lunged into recessions when the pressure of inflation looked too severe. Even a very leaky boat can be temporarily pumped dry, with enough effort. But floundering along on yesterday's answers was becoming increasingly ineffective and unpopular.

The Reagan Revolution

How is the Reagan administration addressing the problems that ended the postwar expansion and led to stagflation? For two of the four fundamental problems the White House offers depressing or dangerous solutions; for the other two they apparently have not understood the questions.

In response to the decline of U.S. power abroad, Reagan proposes his massive military buildup. However, the world has changed enough so that no amount of rearmament will recreate the position of strength the U.S. possessed before 1965. Our drift into Vietnam-style military intervention in Central America is actively opposed by such major allies as France and Mexico. Our nuclear saber-rattling has sparked a European peace movement of unprecedented size; getting tough with the Russians will not whip either Western Europe or the Third World back into line, although Ronald Reagan and the rest of us could easily die trying. And even complete success in projecting U.S. military power abroad would not cure our trade deficit. For that key economic problem, Reagan offers only the cruel hope that lower wages will allow U.S. companies to compete more effectively with imports.

When it comes to energy, Reagan is oblivious to the high cost, in both dollars and environmental damage, of his chosen policy of deregulating domestic oil, coal and gas production. The satisfaction of paying the same high prices to domestic producers instead of to Saudi Arabia will do little for the consumers and industries who are stuck with high fuel bills—and with the dirty air and water. Elsewhere in the energy wars, the president appears to have missed the obituaries for the nuclear power industry, published almost monthly in the business press. While utilities welcome his help in defending existing and partially completed nukes, they are not about to throw good money after bad by actually ordering new ones. In addition, Reagan has set about undoing what little Carter had achieved in promoting energy conservation and alternative energy development.

The decline of autos, highways, suburbs and related areas such as steel and trucking—indeed, the very notion that it matters that a whole set of once strong heavy industries are now dying—seems to have floated right past the Reagan White House. The concept of a conscious policy for reindustrialization scarcely enters the rhetoric of Reaganomics, let alone the reality. As Congressman Gerry Studds said in a different context (he was criticizing military aid to El Salvador), "No one is going to accuse the current leadership of being either the best or the brightest."[8]

Attacking the changing nature of government is of course what Reagan likes best. Was the past shift from military to civilian spending unprofitable for business? Fear not, help is on the way. In fact, reorienting some of civilian manufacturing toward weapons production is the closest thing to an industrial strategy that Reagan has come up with. Have government services and income supports made workers too capable of resisting wage cuts in recessions? There is good news for employers on this front too, as one federal program after another is being forced to wither away. The nineteenth-century version of the trade-off, curing inflation by periodically reducing the working class to starvation wages, may not be as permanently behind us as we once thought.

Thus the reality of Reaganomics consists of rearming the United States and (for all but those at the top) reducing U.S. standards of living. It is a militarily dangerous and socially cruel strategy—and ultimately an unsuccessful one. The growth areas it creates, military hardware and, presumably, luxury goods and services for the newly enriched elite, are far from sufficient to replace the former strengths of the U.S. economy. Its answer to inflation turns out to be a bigger, badder economic slump than any previous administration had dared to try.

In rhetoric, Reaganomics promised a more attractive approach, one which did an outstanding job of addressing the frustrations of the late 1970s. It offered to restore economic growth, to stop inflation without recession, to make everyone better off. Such a pitch was invaluable on the campaign trail in 1980, and can be heard again on the evening news whenever Congress balks at part of the president's program. But the rhetoric only conceals the real agenda of the strange new economics of Ronald Reagan.

CHAPTER 2

Gurus and Flakes:
Friedman and Gilder

Whenever there are great strains or changes in the economic system, it tends to generate crackpot theories, which then find their way into the legislative channels.

— *David Stockman*

The 1970s appeared to be the decade in which conventional economic wisdom declared its intellectual bankruptcy. Consequently the 1980s have opened as the test of the rightwing alternative. The conservative answer to the problems of slow growth and accelerating inflation—as to so many other problems—is to use the incentives of higher profits to coax corporations into better behavior. Any limits on private enterprise, whether by unions, government programs or environmental regulations, are simply social debris that must be swept away to clear the broad path to prosperity.

Cruel as it is in human terms, this position has a certain inner logic. Profits are the difference between a firm's selling price and its costs. So to boost profits and hold down prices at the same time, costs must be slashed. About two-thirds of total corporate revenues are paid out in wages, salaries and fringe benefits; thus labor costs, in particular, must be reduced in order to make it profitable to fight inflation. There are only two ways to cut labor costs: by increasing the amount a worker produces per hour, or by lowering the amount a worker is paid per hour. Productivity (the amount produced per hour) can be raised by new innovations or by old-fashioned speed-up; it is the subject of frequent exhortations by corporate public relations departments. Yet behind the glossy appeals there is widespread doubt that much can be achieved very quickly. In recent years productivity has been stagnant or declining, not rising.

The core of the conservative strategy for fighting inflation, therefore, is fighting wage increases. Again the arguments are compelling, especially if you are sure, as economists and politicians generally are, that your wages are not the ones being discussed. Lower wages and prices will make U.S. goods more competitive abroad, restoring some of the country's lost international strength. One reason why wages do not fall in recessions is the availability of a wide array of government social services and benefits; a rollback of these programs will make workers more insecure, more continuously dependent on employers, more willing to work for less. The funds formerly spent on social welfare can then be diverted to tax cuts for business and for the rich, and to increases in the military budget.

Described in these terms, the conservative program for the economy would have limited popular appeal. In a time of frustration over already declining living standards, there would be little support for blunt advocacy of further cuts in wages and social services, combined with handouts to the rich, as the way to fight inflation.

Described as "Reaganomics," however, this same conservative program has been triumphantly popular. Through the 1980 election and at least the first year of the Reagan administration, millions of people supported what amounted to an attack on their own material well-being. This paradox of democracy is explained by a masterpiece of marketing. The right wing has been vague or misleading about the effects its economic program will have on most people, while emphasizing again and again its claim that growth, creativity, initiative, and above all, personal freedom can come only from the unfettered operation of private enterprise.

Like any successful ideology, this is a sincere belief, not a cynical smokescreen, for many of its advocates. A professional actor and politician like Ronald Reagan may have realized the need for euphemisms and crowd-pleasing lines to sell conservatism to the electorate. But neither he nor anyone else mechanically composed a new theory for the 1980s. Instead, conservatives who were formerly out of tune with the dominant liberal consensus found themselves rapidly acquiring more listeners. The very failures of mainstream economics seemed to legitimize and popularize its longstanding opponents on the right.

Among the works of the newly fashionable ideologues, two bestsellers have appeared expounding two sometimes contradictory strands of conservative economics. Milton Friedman, the leader of the economics profession's "loyal opposition" in more liberal times, has with his wife Rose produced *Free to Choose,* a book dedicated to the proposition that the market is a Good Thing but government is not. George Gilder recently emerged from his well-deserved obscurity on the far right to write *Wealth and Poverty,* a hymn to supply-side economics, the patriarchal family, innovation and (literally) divine irrationality.

The Friedmans and Gilder share many common themes: disgust at the concept of publicly provided social services, scorn for concerns about economic equality and justice, and adoration for the miracles wrought by private business decision-making. They differ in the political myths they use to defend capitalism, and in their prescriptions for economic policy. On the latter point, they represent the two sides of the principal economic debate within the Reagan administration.

Free to Lose

> . . . . you can, if you are an egalitarian, estimate what money income would correspond to your concept of equality. If your actual income is higher than that, you can keep that amount

and distribute the rest to people who are below
that level.[1]

That's just one of the choices open to you in the brave
new economic world foreseen by the Friedmans. There's so
much you could choose to do; there's so much the economy
could do in response to your choices. . . . if only those med-
dlesome government bureaucrats (who never do anything right,
anyway) would unleash the free market and let 'er rip.

For anyone concerned about social and economic justice,
Free to Choose is a dangerous book. It spent months on the
bestseller lists in 1980, curiously enough placed on the non-
fiction side. It is a highly partisan book; Ronald Reagan raves
about it on the jacket flap, while Jimmy Carter and Teddy
Kennedy come under attack in the text. Its message, though,
is being heard more and more by Democrats as well as Republicans.

Its message is nothing less than a redefinition of the word
"freedom." The market offers freedom: if you like Ultra-Glop
toothpaste, no one can force you to buy Presto-Goo instead.
Government, in contrast, means coercion: if you want your
taxes spent on street repairs but a majority of your neighbors
are more concerned about fire protection, your dollars are
enslaved and shipped off to fill the coffers of the fire department
against your will. The book's title and almost every page of the
text hammer home the redefined concepts. Buying and selling
are freedom; voting and planning are slavery.

The market is not only personally liberating, claim the
Friedmans; it also creates the best of all possible economies.
In pursuit of this claim they present one big theory and one
big distortion of reality. The theory, one of the great insights
of the eighteenth century, is the explanation of the way competitive markets work. If consumers suddenly want more tomatoes and less lettuce than before, they will be willing to pay
a higher price for tomatoes as they compete for scarce supplies.
Lettuce, on the other hand, will go partly unsold unless its
price is lowered. Farmers will notice these changes, conclude
there's more money to be made in tomatoes and less in lettuce,
and adjust next year's crop accordingly. The Friedmans, like
Adam Smith before them, find this terribly exciting. You get

exactly the right mix of tomatoes and lettuce every time, with no planning or government regulation required.

The distortion of reality is the assertion that the whole economy can and should work on this principle. The Friedmans simply announce that the biggest businesses, like small farmers deciding between lettuce and tomato crops, are controlled by consumer choices.

> In fact, the people responsible for pollution are consumers, not producers. They create, as it were, a demand for pollution. People who use electricity are responsible for the smoke that comes out of the stacks of the generating plants.[2]

Notice the disappearing trick that is being done here. If the market is so all-powerful that every detail of a large corporation's behavior is a response to consumers' wishes, then the very possibility of corporate power has vanished. Since it is forced to continually respond to your choices, big business is on your side.

> The chief economic function of a department store, for example, is to monitor quality on our behalf. . . . Sears, Roebuck and Montgomery Ward, like department stores, are effective consumer testing and certifying agencies as well as distributors.[3]

Not so with big government. Aside from a few minimal functions such as providing police, military forces and (the Friedmans' favorite) a stable currency, the government should leave everything alone. Social services and programs are undesirable. The preferable alternative is to bring back charities, private philanthropy and reliance on family members.

> The difference between Social Security and earlier arrangements is that Social Security is compulsory and impersonal—earlier arrangements were voluntary and personal. Moral responsibility is an individual matter, not a social matter. Children helped their parents out of love or duty. They now contribute to the support of

someone else's parents out of compulsion and
fear.[4]

Since they believe freedom resides only in the most individual
actions, it is not surprising that the Friedmans view moral responsibility the same way. If nothing that anyone wants or
needs, nothing that makes people feel free, is social in nature,
then no one has the right to make any claims on you. Why
worry about old people, when you can take the money and
run?

Having grasped this thread of an essentially anti-social
understanding of society, it is not hard for the Friedmans to
unravel the justification for most government programs. The
bulk of the book is devoted to cataloguing government activities the Friedmans dislike: "The minimum wage law requires
employers to discriminate against persons with low skills," the
Occupational Safety and Health Administration is "a bureau-
cratic nightmare that has produced an outpouring of complaints," and on and on.

What's Wrong With This Picture?

There are three major flaws in the Friedmans' free market
ideal: the misrepresentations of the nature of corporations, of
people and of government.

The Friedmans' central claim is that corporations, if freed
of government interference, would be forced by the market to
do nothing but carry out consumers' desires. This is vegetable-
stand economics, a far cry from the reality of power wielded
by such giants as Exxon, General Electric and AT&T. It is one
thing to point out that even the biggest firms must eventually
sell their products to someone. It is quite another thing to
allege that multi-billion-dollar corporations' decisions on advertising, plant location, labor relations and environmental
protection are dictated by the will and whims of consumers.

There is no record of the consumer demand for Hooker
Chemical's faulty waste disposal at Love Canal. No Mobil customers have demanded that part of their oil dollars be spent
spewing forth propaganda in newspaper ads. Nor have Exxon
customers insisted on that company's unsuccessful ventures
into the computer and electric motor industries. Telephone
users are not responsible for most operators being female and

most repair personnel being male; coal users do not clamor for more deaths in the mines. Indeed, both the telephone and coal industries continued to thrive in the 1970s despite federal regulations that began to alleviate sex discrimination and on-the-job accidents. The Friedmans may decline to mention it, but corporate power lives on despite them.

If the Friedmans' corporations are strangely weak, their people are implausibly affluent and self-reliant. Crusading for the belief that freedom means shopping, the Friedmans employ a favorite metaphor of economists: "When you vote daily in the supermarket, you get precisely what you voted for, and so does everyone else." There are at least three problems with the supermarket as polling place.

First, some people may ignore the Friedmans' advice and persist in wanting things that don't fit on the shelves. There is no way for a single individual to freely choose mass transit, pollution control, a ban on nuclear power, clean streets, fire protection, guaranteed incomes for senior citizens or other intrinsically social goods and services. Collective choice and government action are required, once it is admitted that people have legitimate social wants and needs.

Second, unlike some other polling places, one person may arrive in the supermarket with ten times as many votes as another. The richer you are, the more you get to say about what consumer goods will be produced. The undemocratic implications of this do not seem to trouble the Friedmans. In fact, they offer an aggressive defense of the virtues of income inequality.

> It is certainly not fair that Muhammad Ali should be able to earn millions of dollars in one night. But wouldn't it have been even more unfair to the people who enjoyed watching him if, in the pursuit of some abstract ideal of equality, Muhammad Ali had not been permitted to earn more. . . . than the lowest man on the totem pole could get for a day's unskilled work on the docks?[5]

Third, when economists talk about "the market," they include the world of work as well as consumption. You are free to go shopping for jobs too, or for places to invest your idle millions. The following statement is supposed to apply to decisions about taking jobs as well as buying toothpaste.

> The key insight of Adam Smith's *Wealth of Nations* is misleadingly simple: if an exchange between two parties is voluntary, it will not take place unless both believe they will benefit from it.[6]

A misleadingly simple insight, indeed. In some exchanges one party is making the voluntary choice to take a minimum-wage job instead of starving, while the other is making the voluntary choice to employ 101 workers instead of 100.

But working people are not a species with whom the Friedmans are terribly familiar or comfortable. Many readers will be surprised to learn that "you can travel from one end of the industrialized world to the other and almost the only people you will find engaging in backbreaking toil are people who are doing it for sport." In a chapter on unions, the first example to be discussed is the American Medical Association, perhaps a group the Friedmans have more social contact with. One lesson drawn from this "union" is that "physicians are among the most highly paid workers in the United States. That status is not exceptional for persons who have benefited from labor unions."

Having distorted the economic roles of corporations and people, the Friedmans do the same for government. Big government is not a plague that fell from the sky to afflict a healthy private economy. It is only in part a response to popular pressures for social programs. In many ways big business needs big government. The Pentagon protects multinational corporations around the world, provides jobs and lucrative weapons contracts and stimulates new technologies such as computers. Highways, fire protection, police and other basic services are necessary to any business. Many regulatory agencies have been "captured" by, and primarily serve the interests of, the industries they are supposed to regulate—as the Friedmans acknowledge. Even social programs may protect business stability by coopting potentially dangerous popular unrest. Such cooptation appeared both politically necessary and economically affordable in the late 1960s and early 1970s; by now, it looks expensive and dispensible.

The Seductive Promise

Strange as they are, the theories in *Free to Choose* have become a force to be reckoned with. Their strength reflects the corresponding weakness of liberalism; the Friedmans at least have a clear, powerful ideal to advocate. In the realm of academic economics, liberals as well as conservatives attempt to impress their students with the theoretical charms of the competitive market. The difference is that liberals are more prone to admit its impossibility and concentrate on empirical description of the economy or debates over minor reforms. Conservatives like the Friedmans are more inclined to demand that reality be clobbered into agreement with their competitive ideals.

In government, the liberal programs and initiatives the Friedmans are attacking really don't work very well. Who, after all, wants to defend the present systems of public education, welfare or Social Security taxes? Rather than reshaping them, though, the Friedmans want to abolish these and many other programs. Clearly, major changes are needed throughout the government apparatus, but the Friedmans propose to throw out the concept of modern plumbing with the bathwater.

The "abolitionist" approach to government programs has a strong popular appeal. Most people feel powerless today, in the face of both government and corporate bureaucracies. Even the recipients of government services are often frustrated, insulted and demeaned by the manner in which the services are provided. *Free to Choose* offers the spurious but seductive promise that, indeed, you could have power over the way things are done, if only the government would let you. In the absence of a more sensible route to participation in making society's major decisions, the Friedmans' promise will appeal to many people.

Doubtless the Friedmans' imagery also appeals to captains of industry. They should find it gratifying to hear themselves described as obedient servants of the public will. Such emphatic denials of the power of big business can only help capitalists in their public relations and political battles. The attack on social programs also fits well with the current corporate agenda. Cutbacks in public services and benefits will make people more dependent on their employers and less able to resist wage cuts in recessions.

Does such political theorizing lead directly to a prescription for managing the economy and reducing inflation? If so, this book doesn't prove it. The "monetarism" for which Milton Friedman is well-known among economists is tacked on almost as an afterthought at the end of *Free to Choose*. In essence it is a convoluted argument for the same old policy of fighting inflation with recessions.

Monetarist theory says that people and businesses spend whatever money they have on hand at a roughly constant rate, called the "velocity of money." If the government allows the total supply of money in the economy to grow more rapidly than the real production of goods and services, spending will also grow faster than production. This means intensified competition for limited supplies of goods and services, leading to price hikes. Therefore, say the Friedmans, "there is only one cure for inflation: a slower rate of increase in the quantity of money."

Only a small fraction of the "money supply" consists of dollar bills, coins and the like. Far more important is the total amount of balances in checking accounts. The Federal Reserve System, as well as directly controlling the production of currency, indirectly controls the expansion of checking account balances. When the Fed tries to apply the Friedmans' cure for inflation, it forces private banks to limit the amount of money they can loan to consumers and businesses. With loan funds in scarce supply, the interest rate shoots up. The monetarist cure for inflation thus translates into high interest rates to discourage borrowing. Because the government is unlikely to stick to "tight money" and high interest rates when it is borrowing money itself to finance the deficit, monetarists also advocate balanced budgets.

There are technical disputes about the monetarist analysis. For example, most economists do not believe that the velocity of money is really constant. More important, though, are the results of monetarism. Balanced budgets and high interest rates lead to recessions. Or, as the Friedmans say, "Unpleasant side effects of the cure are unavoidable." In other words, the monetarist cure for inflation looks very much like the conventional economic policies of the 1970s, fighting price hikes with unemployment. A new jargon in which to talk about it, and a slightly greater emphasis on monetary rather than fiscal policy, do not make recessions any more popular, or any more effective in stopping inflation.

A Modest Proposal

> A state that responds by confiscation and coercion to the inevitable crises . . . . ends by consuming its own people. The rates of taxation climb and the levels of capital decline, until the only remaining wealth beyond the reach of the regime is the very protein of human flesh, and that too is finally taxed, bound, and gagged, and brought to the colossal temple of the state—a final sacrifice of carnal revenue to feed the declining elite.[7]

George Gilder doesn't mince words. Seen through his looking glass, economic controls lead to literal cannibalism. Women earning as much as 80% of male salaries, the situation among blacks today, emasculates the father/provider role, driving men into promiscuous sexuality, drug abuse and all manner of hedonistic squalor. Italians, Poles and black West Indians in this country all earn more than WASPs do. Contact with God determines which small businesses succeed. The average welfare family has a higher income than the average working family.

Indeed, on reading *Wealth and Poverty,* one is struck that the Friedmans, however distortedly and anti-socially, were recognizably describing the planet we all live on. With Gilder one is less sure. His is a world in which there is only one true way to live and prosper: plug your ears against the siren song of free government benefits, form strict patriarchal families and take daring gambles in starting new businesses.

Gilder's world is less crowded than ours. Several categories of people seem to be entirely absent; among them are workers, managers and owners of large corporations. Major capitalist enterprises are uninteresting: "From the point of view of over-

all economic growth and technological innovation, these levi-
athans are of little importance to the economy."[8] Accordingly,
trade unions, routine or dead-end jobs, fortunes or even comfortably affluent salaries deriving from the mainstream of the
U.S. economy have all been banished. Gilderland is the scene
of simpler, wilder adventures.

> The fact is that the United States is probably
> the most mobile society in the history of the
> world. The virtues that are most valuable in it
> are diligence, discipline, ambition, and a
> willingness to take risks. . . . Some 400,000
> new small businesses are started
> annually . . . . Business is not only the best
> route to wealth in America; it is almost the only
> route for those without education. In business,
> moreover, the sky is the limit.[9]

The sky is one limit; bankruptcy is the other. Gilder is actually
aware that the latter is encountered far more often by small
businesses, but prefers not to dwell on that fact until the end
of the book.

The drama of launching new businesses, and the central
role they are said to play in the economy, are at times supposed
to be a description of reality, at other times an ideal, a faith
to which Gilder hopes to convert the reader. Such distinctions
between "is" and "ought" are frequently fuzzed over in *Wealth
and Poverty* since Gilder believes ideas are more real and important than the physical world.

> Marx, however, erroneously located the means
> of production in the material arrangements of
> the society rather than in the metaphysical cap-
> ital of human freedom and creativity. The prob-
> lem of contemporary capitalism lies not chiefly
> in a deterioration of physical capital, but in a
> persistent subversion of the psychological means
> of production—the morale and inspiration of
> economic man (sic). . . .

Or, more tersely if obscurely, "A capitalist system is chiefly
a noosphere, a circuit of ideas and feelings."[10]

A Capital Idea

If wealth is only an idea in noospheric capitalism, why is it an idea that so few of us have gotten? Gilder's answer appears to be that too many people are living in sin. "Indeed, after work the second principle of upward mobility is the maintenance of monogamous marriage and family." A married man "is spurred by the claims of family to channel his otherwise disruptive male aggressions into his performance as a provider for a wife and children."[11] A woman, of course, is supposed to stay home and play Beauty taming the Beast.

The subject of family life is the cue for the grand entrance by the villains of Gilder's psychodrama: government bureaucrats and feminists. Both profane the sanctity of the male provider role by suggesting that women can get along without men. Both undermine "male confidence and authority, which determine sexual potency, respect from the wife and children, and motivation to face the tedium and frustration of daily labor." When a woman receives welfare benefits,

> The man has the gradually sinking feeling that his role as provider, the definitive male activity from the primal days of the hunt through the industrial revolution and on into modern life, has been largely seized from him; he has been cuckolded by the compassionate state.

> His response to this reality is that very combination of resignation and rage, escapism and violence, short horizons and promiscuous sexuality that characterize everywhere the life of the poor . . . . Boys grow up seeking support from women, while they find manhood in the macho circles of the street and the bar or in the irresponsible fathering of random progeny.[12]

Many liberal and radical critics have noted that Aid to Families with Dependent Children (AFDC) encourages the breakdown of families, since its benefits are so much more readily available (in some cases only available) when fathers are absent. Gilder's innovation, aside from nostalgia for the days when women stayed in their place, is his belief that welfare is a comfortable living, seducing hard-working people to a life of indolence and marital separation. He insists that the *average* welfare family of four received close to $18,000 in 1979, somewhat above the median income for the country as a whole. Like many of Gilder's bizarre "facts," this point is documented only by reference to a publication of a right wing think tank—in this case, *The Welfare Industry,* from the Heritage Foundation.

In reality, AFDC averaged $93 per person per month in 1979.[13] For a four-person family that's $4,464 per year. Even with food stamps and Medicaid thrown in, it seems unlikely that the lures of AFDC will attract many families earning $18,000 a year. And, money aside, the well-known degrading treatment of recipients by the welfare system drives most people to find ways off welfare whenever possible.

Back in Gilderland, however, welfare mothers are living high off the hog. The great fear is that millions more will sign up as soon as they hear the good news. The solution is to slash welfare and Medicaid payments, and to pay welfare recipients' rent directly to their landlords, as a further check on wanton living. If the dole can be made sufficiently unpleasant, a task Gilder sees as remaining to be done in the future, then the idle poor will return to strict male-dominated families, ready to board the big escalator upward.

Climb Down From That Pole!

The path to prosperity is threatened by more than the largesse of the welfare bureaucracy. In recent years feminism has reared its head, demanding that women be given equal access to jobs and equal pay. This is unfortunate, because men need the money more than women do.

> The man's earnings, unlike the woman's, will determine not only his standard of living but also his possibilities for marriage and children— whether he can be a sexual man. The man's work thus finds its deepest source in love.[14]

Among blacks, working women earn 80% as much as men, compared to 60% among whites. So Gilder feels the problem is especially serious for blacks. His solution to black poverty, by which he means black male poverty, is to make black women poorer.

> Any increase in the independence of black women, secured both by welfare and by jobs, will only further expand the appalling percentages of black children raised without fathers.

Black men don't even benefit much from government anti-discrimination programs, since they

> are now forced to join an undignified queue with such improbable victims as Yale coeds molested by their tutors, ex-addicts denied reemployment, assistant professors at Smith rejected for tenure, and telephone operators who discover, years later, that what they had always wanted was to climb a pole.[15]

Yet even among black men, discrimination isn't really a problem. Older black workers, in particular, went to inferior schools and hence received diplomas that are "worth" less in the job market. (The astute reader will notice that racism has not entirely vanished in this explanation of wage differentials.) Gilder believes that blacks' lower incomes are entirely explained by differences in age, region of the country, years of schooling and quality of schooling. If only the government would stop carrying on about racism, blacks would forget about it.

> . . . . by cultivating a pervasive expectation of bias and futility, a posture of upward resentment and appeals for rights rather than upward movement and self-reliance, Washington is profoundly damaging the prospects of the black poor. At a time when it is hard to find discrimination anywhere, blacks are being induced to see it everywhere . . . . in a world of decreasing bias, the anticipation of it creates an air of ambivalent resignation and pugnacity unattractive to any employer. Discrimination is not the problem of the American poor.[16]

The answer to poverty couldn't be simpler: quit pretending that racism still exists; clamp down on those irresistible welfare checks; let female earnings sink low enough to rebuild every male ego in sight.

Gilder offers the carrot as well as the stick to the poor. Just keep those families together, keep those male aggressions channeled into economic achievement, and you too can be rich. Follow the example of a Lebanese immigrant family who arrived in Lee, Massachusetts ten years ago, hardly even able to speak English. The father got up at five o'clock every morning, drove a hundred miles to a farming area and bought vegetables. Then the entire family spent the day selling them at a roadside stand. No time for nonsense like school: "All six children were sources of accumulating capital as they busily bustled about the place." Today that family owns the biggest office building in Lee (three stories high), a few stores and some nice clothes. Noticeably lacking from this inspiring tale are any statistics on the percentage of penniless immigrants who own three-story buildings ten years after arrival, though Gilder does point out that two other Lebanese families have opened businesses in western Massachusetts.[17]

The Pleasure of Giving

Gilder's central economic myth is different from the Friedmans'. *Free to Choose* reflects at least an awareness that large corporations are important in the economy. It sticks to the ancient fable of "consumer sovereignty," so well-loved by traditional economists and businessmen: you, the consumer, dictate what businesses must do. *Wealth and Poverty,* on the other hand, claims that you—if you are a clean-living male citizen—can quickly become one of the significant businessmen in the economy.

Corresponding to the difference in myths is a difference in the major rhetorical claims. While the Friedmans stress the notion that shopping is freedom, Gilder is more taken with the idea that investment is giving. He suggests that modern capitalist investment is an updated form of the potlatch custom of the Kwakiutl (native Americans of the northwest) and other traditional societies, a ceremonial process of feasts and gift-giving provided for the entire tribe by one individual at a time.

> The gifts of advanced capitalism in a monetary economy are called investments. . . . Like gifts, capitalist investments are made without a predetermined return. . . . The gifts will succeed only to the extent that they are altruistic and spring from an understanding of the needs of others.[18]

One might wonder whether employees are also involved in giving, since their efforts on the job necessarily "spring from an understanding of the needs of others." But once again, workers scarcely exist except as potential businessmen of the future. One might also doubt that the Kwakiutl retained legal ownership and control over their gifts after giving them, as capitalists do over investments. The metaphor of giving, though, is a staple feature of Gilder's language. Businesses give, the government takes. Social services can thus be described as resting on greed, while investing money is evidence of altruism. Gilder is of course free, like Humpty Dumpty in *Through the Looking-Glass,* to make words mean whatever he wants them to; the reader is warned that normal usage has been left far behind.

Gilder's economic policy proposals flow directly from the need to prevent bad vibes among the gift-givers. He is against all manner of controls on business, just as the Friedmans are. But aside from the suggestion that economic planning leads to cannibalism—Gilder's forays into anthropology seem to have met with rather limited success—he adds nothing important to the Friedmans' attack on government intervention. Where he parts company with traditional conservative thought is in the advocacy of supply-side economics and the rejection of monetarism.

For Gilder, increasing the incentives for businesses to invest is the beginning and the end of economic policy. All other objectives, even fighting inflation, balancing the budget and slowing the growth of the money supply, are secondary. If it will help investment and growth, perhaps a little inflation isn't so bad; after all, Japan had the highest inflation rate in the industrial world after World War II. Inflation is caused by rising real costs, and attempts to choke it off with tight monetary policy may be either futile (since new monetary forms such as money market funds will continually be invented, evading the controls on older forms of money) or disastrous (since high interest rates prevent borrowing and business growth, especially the small business growth Gilder loves so well). In his critique of monetarism and old-fashioned conservative economics, Gilder achieves some quite atypical moments of down-to-earth common sense.

In presenting an alternative, Gilder escapes back into the stratosphere. He is an ardent advocate of supply-side economics, the new school of thought which is contending with traditional conservatism within the Reagan administration. Supply-siders argue that past government policy has overemphasized the "demand side" of the economy. Either by buying things directly, or by giving individuals money to spend, the government helps maintain the demand for goods and services. At the same time, the story goes, increasing taxes (needed to finance all that spending) and regulations have inhibited the "supply side" of the economy, discouraging producers from producing. Thus demand grows faster than supply, and consumers competing for scarce goods and services drive up prices. The solution is to de-emphasize the demand side—cut back government spending—and to stimulate the supply side by reducing the burden of taxes and regulation.

It is one thing to argue that cutting taxes and regulations would have some effect on production and incomes, though possibly a quite small effect. Many economists of varying persuasions would agree with that statement. It is another thing, and the mark of the committed supply-siders, to believe that tax cuts and regulatory rollbacks are *the* necessary and sufficient ingredients to perk up the economy's performance. The debate, in other words, is not about whether supply-side effects exist. It is about whether they are too small to matter, or so big that nothing else matters.

George Gilder is not one to support anything halfheartedly. Nothing could be better than a big tax cut when it comes to inspiring investors to give more of their gifts, he says. Taxes are ruining the business world. A numerical example purports to show how a 10% before-tax rate of profit on a New York City business could dwindle to a 1% after-tax return. While the crushing burden of taxation on business investment had escaped the attention of most economists, it "was manifest to a former football player trained in physical education, Congressman Jack Kemp. . . ."[19]

Tax cuts are magic. Taxpayers win and the government doesn't even have to lose. That's the argument of the infamous Laffer curve, invented by supply-sider Arthur Laffer, which fascinates Gilder, Jack Kemp and others. Imagine that the government has been taxing profits in the widget industry at the rate of 99%; this has of course discouraged businessmen from entering the field, and pre-tax profits might be as low as one million dollars. Now imagine that Ronald Reagan is elected and cuts the tax rate on widget profits to a mere 90%. Everywhere investors rush to reconsider widgetry; new factories open and pre-tax profits may shoot up to two million dollars. The lower tax rate, 90% instead of 99%, has stimulated so much new business that total tax revenues rise (90% of two million is a lot more than 99% of one million).

The widget boom is a perfectly logical abstract possibility; the interesting question is whether it ever occurs in the real world. Gilder simply announces that it is the norm. Why bother investing if the profits will all be taxed away? It's more fun to relax and go sailing instead of doing all that hard, creative work of giving gifts to the economy. It is only one step further to Gilder's mind-boggling conclusion that the low revenues collected from the capital gains tax or the estate tax are evidence that the rates are too high. Slash the rates and capitalists will spend so much less effort on tax avoidance that more money will flow into the treasury.

This, then, is the supply-side faith: tax cuts mean workers will work more; investors will invest more; production will rise. Inflation will be cured by increased production, since when there's more of something its price drops. Some or all (or for true believers like Laffer and Gilder, more than all) of the lost tax revenue will be made up because even though tax rates are lower, taxable incomes are higher. Even government deficits will eventually be eliminated by this magic.

Alas for Gilder and his ilk, there is no reason to think the economy actually works this way, and there is a growing body of evidence that it doesn't. (See Chapter 3.) Numerous studies by economists have failed to find the alleged tremendous response to tax cuts. Ronald Reagan performed a real-life experiment on the economy in the first year of his administration, reaching much the same negative conclusions. Whatever their fondness for rightwing ideologues, investors will not recklessly put their money where Gilder's mouth is. In the absence of the supply-siders' predicted boom in production, a big tax cut looks inflationary. It is therefore accompanied by tight money a la Friedman, with the accompanying tendency toward recession.

Up From Rationality

Details like practicality of proposals, though, are not really Gilder's forte. He has, even more than the Friedmans, a grand, dynamic vision to offer.

> In every economy . . . . there is one crucial and definitive conflict. This is not the split between capitalists and workers, technocrats and humanists, government and business, liberals and conservatives, or rich and poor. All these divisions are partial and distorted reflections of the deeper conflict: the struggle between past and future, between the existing configuration of industries and the industries that will someday replace them.[20]

Go into business and you will not only enrich yourself; you will be part of the march of history, the future becoming the present.

Yet the crudest form of the myth, the notion that every Lebanese immigrant can strike it rich, is too much even for Gilder in the end. In the body of the book, the reality that most small businesses go broke is given occasional embarrassed mention. At the end Gilder returns to muse on this problem more philosophically. Since almost everyone fails, why do so many keep trying? Prudent planners never succeed, since all the details of a new venture can never be nailed down in advance.

> As in choosing a woman, a man must trust his intuition, and act before he can really know . . . . But not all ideas (or women) are true.[21]

The fact that chance governs success, perhaps a defect in some people's eyes, is to Gilder its great strength.

> Because no one knows which venture will suc-
> ceed, which number will win the lottery, a so-
> ciety ruled by risk and freedom rather than by
> rational calculus, a society open to the future
> rather than planning it, can call forth an endless
> stream of invention, enterprise and art.

Life as a lottery is the only system compatible with human
nature: "The reason capitalism succeeds is that its laws accord
with the laws of mind." But by "mind" Gilder no longer means
one individual.

> The mind has access to a higher consciousness,
> sometimes anomalously, after Jung, called a
> *collective unconscious,* sometimes defined as
> God. (emphasis in original)

This "awesome contact with cosmic mystery and power" is the
hidden force determining who wins the lotteries of life. Then,
in a final crescendo, religious faith

> will lead us to abandon, above all, the idea that
> the human race can become self-sufficient, can
> separate itself from chance and fortune in a hu-
> bristic siege of rational resource management,
> income distribution and futuristic planning. Our
> greatest and only resource is the miracle of hu-
> man creativity in a relationship of openness to
> the divine.[22]

In a book packed with bold claims, the assertion that God is
a supply-side economist may win the chutzpah championship.
But it still won't cure inflation.

Myths and Policies

The more that people understand it, the less popular the
right-wing economic program is likely to be. The "Robin Hood-
in-reverse" flavor of taking from the poor to give to the rich
and to the military is no coincidence, no regrettable necessity
forced on us by the requirements of fiscal responsibility. It is
essential to the conservative strategy of fighting inflation by
boosting profits and holding down wages.

There are some things that can't be talked about in plain
English, however. Ideologues like the Friedmans and Gilder

play the vital role of making the destruction of social welfare programs look attractive to the people who benefit from them, of preparing a broad consensus for policies that will weaken the economic position of most working people. It is done with myths about the merits of capitalism, and with policies that purport to solve the economy's problems.

The myths offered by the two bestsellers of conservative economics are compatible, if different in emphasis. On the one hand, big business is your obedient servant. The mini-decisions you make when you go shopping command the heights of the economy. Shopping is what freedom is all about, unlike government, which involves compromises and the possibility of being outvoted. On the other hand, you are potentially one of the important businessmen in the economy (or his wife, as the case may be). Investment is giving, the creative, altruistic act that makes things go. You too can do it! All it takes is hard work, patriarchal and monogamous families, willingness to gamble against ridiculous odds, refusal to listen to claptrap about government benefits, and mystical belief in a profoundly irrational deity. Gilder's unique accomplishment, aside from reminding us of the threat of cannibalism, is to blend several apparently disparate elements of New Right politics: anti-feminism, fundamentalist religion and supply-side economics are revealed to be intimately connected, at least in one writer's view.

When it comes to policy, the two positions are more sharply opposed. Both agree on the evisceration of the welfare state, but beyond that one wants a new wrinkle on the old policy of tight money and recessions, while the other advocates another one of those daring gambles. How much will you bet that a giant tax cut for the rich is the magical answer to restoring growth and prosperity? As it turns out, Ronald Reagan has been willing to bet much of his political reputation on it, although he has somewhat covered himself with continuing use of the old policies as well.

CHAPTER 3

For the Taxpayer Who Has Everything

It is time to create new jobs, to build and rebuild industry, and give the American people room to do what they do best. And that can only be done with a tax program which provides incentives to increase productivity for both workers and industry. . . .

Unlike some past tax "reforms," this is not merely a shift of wealth between different sets of taxpayers. This proposal for an equal reduction in everyone's tax rates will expand our national prosperity, enlarge national incomes, and increase opportunities for all Americans.

—Ronald Reagan, February 18, 1981

The President is wrong on the two most important points about his tax cut. It *is* a shift of wealth between different income groups, giving more to those who already have the most. And it is not causing much of an increase in productivity or an expansion in national prosperity. The failure of the tax cut to

39

transform the economy is already widely recognized in Washington, creating the impetus for harsher measures such as budget cuts and tight monetary policy.

One of Reagan's most popular campaign promises was the 30% across-the-board tax cut. Scaled down to 23%, it was passed by Congress in August of 1981. Most people, failing to understand the intricacies of the income tax system, thought this meant that everyone would pay 30%, or later 23%, less in income taxes. Even if that were the case, it would still favor the rich; but in reality the tax cut is even more biased than a true across-the-board reduction would be.

How could cutting everyone's taxes by the same percentage favor one group over another? A numerical example may help clarify the issue. Consider the effects of a 23% reduction in income taxes on two hypothetical families. The richer family has an income of $60,000 and pays $18,000 in income taxes, leaving an after-tax income of $42,000. The average family has an income of $20,000 and pays $2,000 in taxes, leaving $18,000 after taxes. (These are approximately the taxes that a family of four taking the standard deduction paid in 1980). A 23% tax cut is worth $4,140 to the rich family, increasing their after-tax income by about 10%. For the average family a 23% tax cut is worth only $460, less than a 3% increase in after-tax income.

An across-the-board cut is tilted toward the rich because the income tax is a "progressive" tax: the higher your income, the greater the percentage it takes. In our example, the rich family was paying 30% of its income, while the average family was paying only 10%, before the tax cut. So the tax cut gave the rich family 23% of 30% of its before-tax income, while it gave the average family only 23% of 10% of its income. This sort of bias is not an inevitable feature of all income tax cuts. It would be easy to cut tax rates more sharply for lower-income groups.

It would be equally possible to cut other taxes which fall most heavily on low- and middle-income taxpayers. The Social Security tax, for instance, takes a bigger bite out of many people's paychecks than does the income tax. Social Security takes a constant percentage out of your wages, salary or self-employment income, up to a ceiling ($32,400 in 1982). It takes nothing from other forms of income, such as interest or dividends, and it takes nothing from the part of your earnings (if any) above the ceiling. This is a "regressive" tax: people below the ceiling pay a higher percentage of their incomes to Social Security taxes than people above it. An across-the-board cut in Social Security taxes would therefore return a greater percentage of income to people below the ceiling. This alternative seems to have escaped the notice of the White House tax-cutters. On the other hand, estate and gift taxes, paid almost exclusively by the rich, have been all but abolished under Reagan.

Biased as an across-the-board cut in income taxes would be, the tax cut adopted in 1981 is even worse. One reason is that this tax cut, unlike most past ones, fails to increase the size of the personal exemptions or standard deduction. A second reason is that the very rich get more than a 23% tax cut, and get it sooner than the rest of us. Both of these effects will be easier to understand after a quick review of the nuts and bolts of the income tax system.

The IRS allows you to exempt $1,000 of income for yourself, plus another $1,000 for each dependent, from any income tax. Then, if you do not itemize deductions, the next chunk of income—the standard deduction, or, in IRS newspeak, the "zero bracket amount"—is also yours to keep. For a married couple filing jointly, the standard deduction is $3,400; for a single individual it is $2,300.

After that, unless you qualify for any of the more esoteric exemptions and exclusions, you begin paying the IRS. In 1980, before the Reagan cuts, a married couple paid 14% of the first $2,100 above exemptions and deductions, 16% of the next $2,100, 18% of the next $4,300, and so on. As income rose the tax rate increased through fifteen steps, or tax brackets, finally peaking at a top rate of 70% on income (after exemptions and deductions) above $212,000. For a single taxpayer the brackets start at lower points; 1980's top rate of 70% was paid on income above $106,000.

As you move into higher brackets, you don't pay the higher rate on your whole income—only on the part which falls into each bracket. A family with $250,000 income would have been described as being "in the 70% bracket" in 1980, but still got the regular exemptions and deductions, paid only 14% on their next $2,100, and so on through all the brackets. Only on the part of their income, after deductions and exemptions, above $212,000 did they pay the IRS 70%.

The system of exemptions, deductions and rising rates in higher brackets makes the income tax quite progressive. Loopholes aside, it is structured to take a larger percentage out of big incomes than out of small ones. But that same structure has a perverse effect in times of inflation. If your before-tax income rises just fast enough to keep up with inflation, your taxes will go up even faster as more of your income is pushed into higher brackets. Known as "bracket creep," this phenomenon is quite important; at 1980 tax rates every 10% increase in income produced a 15% to 16% increase in income taxes.

At first glance the Reagan tax cut looks like the answer to bracket creep. After all, the rates in each bracket are being reduced. But the tax cut does nothing about the form of bracket creep most serious for those on the bottom. For lower-income people the rates in each bracket are less important than the size of the exemptions and deductions. The failure to increase exemptions and deductions in a time of inflation means that a decreasing fraction of your income is free from tax. To the very poor this means a tax increase.

Imagine a two-parent family of four making $10,000 in 1980. They get four personal exemptions of $1,000 each and the standard deduction of $3,400, for a total of $7,400 of tax-free income. Only $2,600, about a quarter of their income, is subject to tax.

Now suppose that prices will rise only 35% from 1980 to 1984 (the optimistic prediction made by the White House in early 1981). If the family exactly keeps up with inflation they will make $13,500 in 1984. But they will still get only $7,400 of tax-free income. They now have $6,100, closer to half of their income, subject to tax.

The result is that, despite the tax cut, their taxes rise much faster than inflation. In 1980 they pay $374, or 3.7% of their income; in 1984 they pay $749, or 5.5% of their income. Bracket creep is alive and well at the lower end of the income distribution.

The failure to increase exemptions and deductions affects everyone, not just the poor. But at higher income levels it is of smaller relative importance, and is balanced or outweighed by the cuts in tax rates. Using the same assumption, family income just keeping up with 35% inflation, Table 1 shows families making $20,000 to $40,000 in 1980 pay roughly the same percentage of their income in taxes in 1980 and 1984, while $50,000 families pay a little bit lower percentage at the end of Reagan's term than at the beginning.

TABLE 1: THE INCOME TAX BURDEN BEFORE AND AFTER THE REAGAN CUTS

	1980		1984
Income	*Taxes as a Percentage of Income*	*Income*	*Taxes as a Percentage of Income*
$10,000	3.7%	$13,500	5.5%
$20,000	11.3%	$27,000	11.5%
$30,000	16.5%	$40,500	16.6%
$40,000	17.4%	$54,000	17.4%
$50,000	21.3%	$67,500	20.6%
$100,000	33.7%	$135,000	30.1%
$250,000	48.6%	$337,500	38.9%

Notes: All taxes are for a married couple filing jointly with four personal exemptions. Those at the lowest three income levels are assumed to take the standard deduction in both years. All others are assumed to claim itemized deductions equal to 10% of their incomes in both years (the assumed level of deductions used by the Census Bureau in similar tables). The 1980–1984 comparisons assume that in those four years everyone's income will rise by 35%, the rate of inflation forecast for the period by the Reagan administration in early 1981.

Sources: IRS, *Form 1040 General Instructions, 1980,* Schedule Y; and *Economic Recovery Tax Act of 1981,* U.S. House of Representatives Report 97–215, p.6.

For those even higher up, the fruits of the tax cut are even juicier. This may have been the point all along. As David Stockman said about the Kemp-Roth bill (the original proposal on which the 1981 tax cut was based),

> The hard part of the supply-side tax cut is dropping the top rate from 70 to 50 percent—the rest of it is a secondary matter. The original argument was that the top bracket was too high, and that's having the most devastating effect on

the economy. Then, the general argument was
that, in order to make this palatable as a political matter, you had to bring down all the brackets. But, I mean, Kemp-Roth was always a
Trojan horse to bring down the top rate.

In the lower and middle tax brackets the rates are being cut
gradually, taking until 1984 to reach levels 23% below those
of 1980. But at the top the rates have been cut further and
faster. All tax brackets have been reduced to no more than
50% as of 1982. This ceiling has no effect on the first eleven
of the fifteen tax brackets, covering your family's first $82,000
above exemptions and deductions. For the next two brackets
the immediate cut to 50% means that the eventual 23% reduction is achieved faster than at lower incomes. And for the
top two brackets, applying only to income beyond your first
$159,000, the rates have been reduced by 26% and 29%, all
in 1982. The table shows the immense windfall this produces;
continuing the assumption of 35% income growth, a family
that received $250,000 in 1980 paid almost ten percentage
points less in income taxes by 1984. (Postponing or cancel-
ling the later installments of the tax cut, as some members of
Congress have proposed, would cause even greater inequity. The
cut in the top rates would survive unscathed, while the cut in the
lower rates would be lessened.)
    In summary, the individual income tax cut adopted in 1981
is inequitable in three major ways. First, even if it were, as is
widely believed, an equal percentage reduction in everyone's
income tax, it would still give a greater percentage increase in
after-tax income to the rich. Second, the failure to raise the
personal exemption and standard deduction will mean a tax
increase for many poor people. Finally, the changes in tax rates
are explicitly more generous to the very rich.
    After 1984 a different kind of change is scheduled to take
place. The rates in each tax bracket will remain fixed, but the
income levels at which the brackets begin will be increased
each year to keep up with inflation. The personal exemption
and standard deduction will be tied to inflation as well. This
will prevent the income tax structure from becoming any more
tilted toward the rich, and will finally eliminate bracket creep.

Raising the exemptions, deduction and brackets along with inflation will tend to freeze the relative distribution of the tax burden at the point reached in 1984. At that point the income tax will weigh much more heavily on the poor, and more lightly on the rich, than it did in 1980.

Bitter Medicine, or Just Bitter?[1]

The biases of the tax cut are a sufficient rebuttal to the alleged populism of Reaganomics. There is no basis for the notion that everyone will benefit equally from the cut. But this does not deal with the dramatic supply-side effects said to be expected from the tax cut. Lower tax rates are supposed to increase the supply of labor and capital by inspiring us all to work more, save more and invest more. Productivity, profits, growth and employment will soar; eventually the deserts will bloom. Perhaps inequity in the short run is an unavoidable side effect of a policy that will get the economy growing again, to everyone's long-run benefit.

Will it work? Will supply-side prosperity trickle down? Is it true that, in the words of John F. Kennedy—frequently quoted by supply-side economists today—"a rising tide lifts all boats"? Or is Walter Heller, chairman of the Council of Economic Advisors under Kennedy, closer to the mark in saying, "Relying on huge supply-side responses to Kemp-Roth tax cuts would be tantamount to bolting the door against inflation with a boiled carrot"?

With apologies to readers who like suspense stories, the conclusion of the following pages will be that the evidence overwhelmingly disagrees with the supply-siders. There are three main areas in which tax cuts are alleged to stimulate the economy: in increasing the amount of work, the amount of savings and the amount of investment being done. In each of these areas the supply-siders have very little ground to stand on.

In the textbook fable of economics, the amount of work that is done depends on workers' individual choices between labor and leisure. The "price" of an hour of leisure is the income given up by not working for that hour, or in other words, the take-home pay that would be received for an additional hour of work. The higher the price of leisure becomes, the more workers will choose labor rather than leisure, and work additional hours. So cuts in tax rates, by raising take-home pay, will induce people to put in more time at work. Implausible as it may sound, this really is the supply-side theory about how to stimulate the supply of labor.

Even in the realm of textbook economics there is a problem with this argument. There are two conflicting effects of an increase in hourly take-home pay. On the one hand some people will be inspired to work more, willing to give up another hour at the beach for $8 but not for $6. On the other hand some people will find that they can now make enough to live on with fewer hours of work, and choose to spend more time at the beach. (Textbooks call these the "substitution effect" and the "income effect" respectively.) There is no way to determine in the abstract which effect will be larger.

In the real world, almost no one is invited to decide exactly how many hours to work, let alone being free to change that decision every time tax rates are altered. Industrial jobs that involve overtime typically give workers little or no choice about how much overtime to work. Most other jobs have hours rigidly fixed in advance. The world of free-lancers, consultants, shop-keepers and other self-employed people who control their own hours is a small part of the labor force.

The only way to make sense of the textbook fable is to interpret it as describing choices about the number of jobs being done. Some people can postpone retirement, work second jobs or switch from part-time to full-time employment. Most important, some families can increase the number of family members working outside the home.

Yet there is less room left for increasing the number of workers than there used to be. More than 90% of men between the ages of 20 and 55 are in the labor force (either holding or actively seeking paid employment); many of the others are enrolled in higher education, or sick or disabled. In the same age range, more than 60% of women are in the labor force; while there can be some further increase, the lack of adequate child care (a worsening problem thanks to current budget cuts) makes it unlikely that both women and men can work outside the home at the rates that men do today.

Moreover, there are millions of people already looking for work but unable to find it; since the labor force is around 100 million, each percentage point of the unemployment rate represents a million jobseekers. Employment is readily available only for those with certain scarce skills. Unless a tax cut can tap hitherto unknown reserves of experienced welders, biochemists and computer programmers, there is no reason to think higher take-home wages will cause higher employment.

Many economists have done statistical studies of the effect of after-tax wages on the amount of work people do. Most studies agree that for men a wage increase leads to a slight *decrease* in hours worked; in the textbook terms, the income effect is slightly greater than the substitution effect. Estimates of the effect of a 10% wage hike on men range from no change to a 4% decrease in hours worked. Among women higher wages stimulate more work; a 10% wage hike may produce an 8% or 9% increase in hours worked by women, though estimates as low as a 1% decrease and as high as a 20% increase have been published. Combining the results for men and women, a recent review of the economic literature concluded that a 10% wage increase probably would prompt a 1.5% increase in total hours of work.[2]

So consider an ideal world, in which unemployment is low enough that people can readily get jobs when they want to, and inflation is slow enough so that bracket creep is not a problem. In this ideal world, imagine that an across-the-board cut of 23% in all tax rates is enacted. That cut might mean a 7% increase in hourly take-home pay for any additional hours of work (at least, it would have meant that for the average real-world family in 1980). Using the combined male/female estimate from the economic literature, a 7% pay increase would lead to a 1% increase in hours worked. Under ideal conditions, that is to say, Reagan's tax cut might stimulate the people of the United States to do 1% more labor. In the real world, where high unemployment and bracket creep interfere with even this modest supply-side effect, the impact of a 23% tax cut on the supply of labor may for all practical purposes be ignored.

The supply-side theory does not pin all its hopes on increases in the supply of labor. Tax cuts are supposed to stimulate more savings as well; more savings means more funds that businesses can borrow for expansion. While most of us are agonizing over the choice between labor and leisure, the rich are debating the merits of saving for the future vs. immediate consumption. (Actually, in the textbooks everyone makes this choice, too; but in reality only the rich have significant-sized savings.) The theory of the two choices is exactly parallel: the "price" of consuming now is the interest foregone by not saving the money. A tax cut gives savers a higher after-tax interest rate, helping to tip the balance toward saving.

One theoretical problem with this analysis is, again, the clash between the substitution effect and the income effect. Higher after-tax interest rates will inspire some wealthy individuals to save more, while others will reach their desired level of interest income with less savings than before, and spend more on caviar instead of bonds. Studies of the effect of changing interest rates on savings have yielded ambiguous and inconclusive results; most economists do not believe there is any proven effect. A controversial 1978 study, often cited by supply-siders, claimed to find a big effect of interest rates on savings. But other economists have found many flaws in the study, and its result is not widely accepted.[3]

The importance of providing incentives to savers, however, is firmly embedded in the 1981 tax cut. The rich receive not only the benefit of the tilt in the new tax rates as described above; they also get several specific new loopholes for certain types of savings. You can now put up to $2,000 a year into a tax-free Individual Retirement Account (IRA). No money can be withdrawn from an IRA (without paying a stiff penalty) until you reach age 59½. You pay no taxes on the amounts you put in, and on the interest received, until you withdraw it—at which time you will likely have a lower income, and hence fall into a lower tax bracket, than in your working years.

Another new loophole was the misnamed "All-Savers" program, announced with great fanfare in late 1981. Special one-year savings bonds were issued, on which the first $1,000 interest per person was tax-free. The catch was that the interest rate on these bonds was well below the market rate, making them worthwhile only if you were in a high tax bracket. People below $30,000–$40,000 in income, in other words most people, did better putting whatever savings they had into higher-interest but taxable alternatives such as money market funds.

Yet another egalitarian loophole allows everyone, rich and poor alike, to receive $750 of public utility company dividends tax-free so long as the money is reinvested in the utility's stocks. Such a specific pork-barrel provision will undoubtedly boost reinvestment in the utility industry. But that is a far cry from concluding that savings throughout the economy will increase. The utilities' gain might come at the expense of lower reinvestment in other industries.

The same question can be raised about all the incentives: are they adding to savings or just taking money out of one form of savings and putting it into another? A friend of mine who has some savings says that he is of course putting $2,000 into an IRA to take advantage of the tax break—but he is also putting $2,000 less into his other savings. When he does this, he no longer pays taxes on that $2,000. If he is in the 50% tax bracket, the U.S. Treasury loses $1,000, and the federal deficit increases by that amount.

This example leads to one of the ultimate ironies of supply-side incentives. Tax loopholes for savers are justified by the claim that they will increase the supply of savings available for business to borrow; in fact, the loopholes probably decrease the savings available to the private sector, because they boost the federal deficit. When my friend moves $2,000 into an IRA, the supply of private savings is unchanged, but the amount the federal government has to borrow has increased by $1,000. So the amount of private savings available for business borrowing has actually fallen by $1,000.

Overall, the incentives for savers in the 1981 tax law are expected to cost the government $8 billion a year in lowered tax revenues by 1986. This means the government will be borrowing $8 billion more than it would have in the absence of the incentives. So the question is, will the incentives increase private savings by $8 billion? The answer appears to be "no." Even accepting many of the supply-siders' own assumptions, it can be shown that tax incentives for savings will usually increase the deficit, and government borrowing, faster than they increase savings. (The calculations are too lengthy to present here.)[4]

With this set of loopholes, the supply-siders have achieved just the opposite of their announced intentions. While putting another $8 billion into some already stuffed pockets, they have likely made less, not more, money available for businesses to borrow and invest.

The Corporate Income Tax: R.I.P.

Even if the savings incentives somehow were to work, they would be of little relevance to boosting business investment. Savings by individuals have always been a relatively minor source of corporate funds. In 1979, for instance, personal savings were $86 billion, while corporations' own funds available for investment (profits remaining after taxes and dividend payments, plus depreciation allowances) totalled $313 billion. Moreover, $79 billion was invested in housing in 1979, almost equal to the volume of personal savings.[5] Textbook mythology asserts that individual household decisions about savings provide the funds for business investment; it would be a closer approximation of reality to say that household savings finance housing, and corporate funds finance corporate investment.

The supply-siders did not forget the corporations at tax-cutting time. To begin with, various tidbits are tossed into some of the usual hungry mouths; new exemptions from the windfall oil profits tax, to cite just one example, will be worth over $3 billion annually by 1986. On the subject of the new loopholes for particular corporate interests, it is hard to be more emphatic than David Stockman.

> Do you realize the greed that came to the forefront? The hogs were really feeding. The greed level, the level of opportunism, just got out of control.

The main course offered to the business world as a whole, though, is much bigger than the loopholes for particular industries. Known in the jargon of official Washington as "capital cost recovery provisions," the principal corporate tax cut will cost the Treasury $53 billion a year by 1986, and far more in later years. It consists of changes in the tax treatment of depreciation, increases in the investment tax credit, and a new loophole for leased equipment—matters which require another detour through the workings of the tax laws before they can be explained.

Imagine for a moment that you are a businessman trying to avoid paying taxes. The corporate income tax takes a percentage of your profits, which are the difference between your sales revenues and your costs. The more you pad your costs, the lower your reported profits, and your taxes, will be. Depreciation is one of the easiest costs to pad.

Suppose you have just bought a machine which will wear out in ten years. You need to save one-tenth of the cost of the machine each year, so that you can afford to replace it in ten years. This is a genuine cost of doing business, and it is the idea behind depreciation allowances. The IRS allows you to call that amount of savings a (tax-free) cost, rather than a (taxable) part of profits.

But the lifetime of a machine is often hard to predict in advance. The shorter you can claim the machine's lifetime will be, the sooner you can set aside the cost of the machine into your tax-free depreciation allowance. Getting this money exempted from tax sooner rather than later can be worth quite a lot to you in a time of inflation and high interest rates.

IRS rules governing the rate at which depreciation allowances can be taken have long been the focus of intense business lobbying. While these rules have become steadily more generous to corporate taxpayers, all past tax laws preserved at least some attempt at determining the actual productive life of business assets, and tied depreciation schedules to those lifetimes. In 1981 the corporate community and its elected representatives had a better idea. Why not pick some very short lifetimes and arbitrarily apply them to all assets?

The result is a system that allows faster depreciation than anyone would have dreamed possible just a few years ago. There are now four categories of property. Cars, trucks, research equipment, older racehorses and other short-lived apparatus can be depreciated over three years. Most other machinery and equipment, younger racehorses, farm buildings and petroleum storage facilities are considered to last five years. (Under the previous law some equipment had a tax lifetime as long as 36 years.) Most other buildings and railroad cars are assigned a ten-year lifetime, except for most public utility property, which is assumed to endure for all of fifteen years. (Previously some buildings had to be depreciated over 60 years.) In almost every case these new figures are ludicrously shorter than the expected useful life of the assets involved. Thus the tax-free depreciation allowances can be built up long before the buildings and equipment physically wear out, amounting to a big tax break.

An additional sweetener sprinkled on top was the increase in the investment tax credit. This credit lets businesses deduct from their taxes a percentage of the price of most new investments. The new rates—a 6% credit for assets in the three-year depreciation category, and 10% in all other categories—are an increase for many, though not all, assets. In addition, petroleum storage facilities and leased railroad cars are for the first time eligible for investment tax credits.

The combination of investment tax credits and fast depreciation will work wonders in reducing a company's tax bill. But it does nothing for businesses that are already paying no taxes, either because they are losing money or because they qualify for more than enough loopholes. The tax cut of 1981 addresses this glaring inequity by introducing a brand new scam, essentially allowing companies to buy and sell tax breaks by pretending to lease equipment to each other.

If this deal were extended to personal taxes, it might look like this. You get a $1,000 personal exemption for each of your children, but if you are too poor to owe any taxes, the exemption is worth nothing to you. Suppose you find someone in the 50% tax bracket, for whom the same exemption is worth $500 a year, and have that person legally adopt your child for the next 20 years. At the same time you sign a contract establishing that despite the adoption, you will retain all rights and responsibilities for actually raising your child for the next 20 years. The richer person, who saves $500 a year in taxes in the bargain, will be willing to pay you some part of his savings. Nothing has changed about your actual relationship to the child; no one loses but the Treasury. If you are an individual doing this with children, it is called fraud. If you are a railroad doing it with boxcars, it is absolutely legal thanks to Ronald Reagan's tax cut.

The opportunity to transfer tax breaks through phony leasing arrangements will ensure that the generous new investment tax credits and depreciation allowances eventually end up on the books of the corporations that "need" them the most. (Imagine all the children in the country ending up on the tax returns of people in the highest tax bracket.) Any company that is still paying income taxes a few years from now should hire a new accountant. The corporate income tax, which had already shrunk from 29% of federal revenue in 1955 to 15% in 1979, will all but vanish by 1990.

If high taxes have been choking off business investment, as the supply-side enthusiasts believe, then it would be hard to imagine anything better than the 1981 tax cut for perking up the economy. Yet here, as with savings incentives, economic studies do not show convincing evidence for the influence of tax rates on investment decisions. Several recent surveys of economic research have concluded that tax rates and other factors affecting the availability and cost of funds are all less important than demand in determining investment. In plain English, the studies seem to show that businesses are willing to invest when they see growing markets for their products, and reluctant to spend money, regardless of tax incentives, when they don't see markets.

In real life the business world appears to agree more with the results of these studies than with the hopes of the supply-siders. In the months immediately following the adoption of the tax cut, the economy sank into recession, due in part to a drop in business investment. As *Business Week* observed in November 1981, events were more in line with the views of John Maynard Keynes, the original "demand-side" theorist.

> The investment slump has to be deeply disturbing to the Administration's supply-side theorists. In their view of the world, business should already be responding to the new incentives provided by the tax cuts retroactive to the beginning of the year. Instead, companies seem to be acting on a Keynesian premise that investment plans respond mainly to a surge in

demand that pushes up operating rates. It is still
too early to give a final grade to the supply-side
view of the investment process. But it is clear
that the theory has flunked the mid-term.[6]

Even the few businesses that continued to prosper in the recession did not boost their spending plans because of tax breaks.
According to Ben Heineman, chairman of Northwest Industries, a profitable manufacturing conglomerate,

> with or without the tax bill we would have done
> what we did in 1981 and what we plan to do in
> 1982. One can spend money on men and ma-
> terials only at a given rate. Beyond that it be-
> comes foolish.[7]

While the tax cut has produced no measurable increase
in spending on new physical assets, it has given business larger
profits to play with. For example, the steel industry, badly in
need of modernization, is said to be spending less than $4
billion a year on its plants and equipment. Yet U.S. Steel was
able to celebrate the first anniversary of the Reagan administration by spending more than $6 billion to acquire Marathon
Oil. Such speculative pursuits will be all that the business tax
cut inspires, as long as the prospects for new productive investment remain bleak.

What Next?

The failure of supply-side incentives is no longer exactly
news. In the absence of the promised surge in production and
incomes, the big tax cut has simply led to a big deficit—to the
embarrassment of conservative Republicans who have always
made a shibboleth of balanced budgets.

To the hard-core advocates of supply-side theory, the
problem is that taxes were not cut fast enough. Perhaps if we
had had the whole 23% tax cut in the first year, the deserts
would be blooming after all. Or, in an even less plausible
variation, perhaps what supply-side policy really needed was
a return to the gold standard—an alternative which would
either lead straight to depression, or, more likely, prove entirely unworkable.[8]

More pragmatic administration policymakers, faced with inescapable evidence that they were, indeed, flunking the mid-term, scrambled in different directions to catch up before the final. Some searched for ever-deeper budget cuts—but the sheer size of the 1981 tax breaks, $150 billion a year by 1984, over $250 billion by 1986, dwarfs the results achieved by David Stockman's budget-cutting orgies. Others advocated "revenue enhancements," or, as they are known outside the nation's capital, tax increases. It is interesting to note that while the Reagan tax cut gave the greatest gains to wealthy individuals and to businesses, the "enhancements" proposed by his aides, such as higher taxes on gasoline, tobacco and alcohol, hit hardest at the poor. Still, the chief himself appears to be dead-set against any substantial tax increases.

Thus the mushrooming government deficit adds to inflationary pressures (see Chapter 1). In Reagan's first year, as in Carter's last one, the government felt compelled to attack inflation with disastrously high interest rates. It has now been demonstrated that administrations from either major party, using either of two different styles of rhetoric, can bring the economy grinding to a halt with tight enough monetary policies. Either way, it turns out to be particularly disastrous to those industries, such as housing and autos, where sales are most dependent on credit.

There appeared to be no alternative for the Reagan administration, however. Without the monetary crunch there was no way to reconcile the president's strong commitments to reducing inflation, to slashing taxes and to boosting the nation's military spending.

CHAPTER 4

The Price of War

. . . the second half of the Administration's program to revitalize America.
—Defense Secretary Caspar Weinberger

. . . nothing less than a conscious commitment to beat our plowshares into swords.
—Congressman Ronald Dellums

We will soon be spending much, much more than we used to preparing for war. At a time when severe cutbacks are being forced on almost all civilian agencies, the Pentagon is being offered annual budget increases of 7% to 9% above the rate of inflation. The numbers are numbingly large; Ronald Reagan wants to spend $1.5 *trillion* on the military over five years, increasing the Defense Department share of the federal budget from 24% in 1981 to 32% in 1984.[1]

The popularly accepted reason for this change, of course, is The Soviet Threat. As in the 1950s and early 1960s, many people in the United States have been convinced that our country is in danger—in which case, expensive as it may be, the military buildup would seem to have a powerful rationale. Discussion of the Pentagon budget must therefore begin with questions of security. Are the Russians really coming? Do we need our present level of armaments, and more, to make us safe in today's world?

The Balance of Terror

The most basic military reality is the nuclear balance of terror. Either the U.S. or the U.S.S.R. could, if it chose to, bomb the other side back into the Stone Age, as a U.S. general once advocated during the Vietnam war. We are, in fact, safely in the lead in this particular race; we have about 10,000 strategic nuclear weapons ("strategic" means long-range ones capable of hitting the opposing superpower) and our NATO allies have about another 1,000, against the Soviet Union's 7,000. But both sides have more than enough.

In the past, military planners assumed that the very balance of terror would provide a grim assurance of peace. The doctrine known as "mutual assured destruction" (MAD) said in effect that since both sides know they would be destroyed by a major war, neither side will start one. Then, barring a computer malfunction in a warning system or the ascent to power of a madman on one side or the other (events which unfortunately are not at all impossible), we are more or less safe.

The advocates of a new buildup in nuclear weaponry claim that MAD is no longer valid. A "window of vulnerability" is supposed to be opening in the late 1980s—a period in which the Soviet Union will have the ability to launch a crippling "first strike," taking us by surprise and destroying so many of our weapons that we would be unable to mount a devastating counterattack. However, such claims ignore the realities of the massive destructive capacity we currently possess.

U.S. nuclear weapons are divided into a "triad"; some are carried on bombers, some on submarines and some on land-based missiles. The triad guarantees that even if two of these types of weapons are somehow destroyed, the third will still be able to flatten the Soviet Union. Under Ronald Reagan, each leg of the triad is being upgraded, at great expense.

Although billions are being spent on the B-1, people outside the Air Force hierarchy increasingly believe that manned bombers are obsolete in an age of faster missiles and antiaircraft weapons. The other two legs of the triad, though, are for all practical purposes invulnerable.

Submarines carry about half of U.S. strategic nuclear weapons. There is no known way to locate moving submarines in the open seas, nor is one expected to be developed anytime soon. In the 1960s Robert MacNamara, then Secretary of Defense, estimated that the missiles on just five U.S. submarines could destroy 59% of Soviet industry and cause an immediate 37 million deaths, nearly twice the Soviet losses in all of World War II.[2] At any time we have at least 20 nuclear-armed submarines at sea, so this destructive capacity would survive even if three-fourths of our subs were sunk in an enemy attack.

One of the statistics which is supposed to scare us into spending more on defense is that the Soviet Union has more submarines than we do. But ours run more quietly (making them harder to detect), can go longer without refueling and spend less of their time in port for maintenance. The U.S. is well ahead in antisubmarine warfare as well.[3] Still, even the smaller number of Soviet submarine-based weapons remain invulnerable to U.S. attack, and are sufficient to incinerate much of the United States. Mutual assured destruction is alive and well under water.

Our land-based missiles, the ones on which the window of vulnerability is supposed to be opening, are in reality almost as secure as the submarines. We have just over 1,000 missiles in concrete-reinforced underground silos, each of which could only be destroyed by a nuclear blast falling within a few hundred feet. It is because of the danger of such an attack that we "need" to add the MX missile to our arsenal.

Yet an attack which simultaneously destroys nearly all of the 1,000 missiles in their silos is almost impossible to imagine. The attacking Soviet missiles would encounter the problem of "fratricide"—the first ones to explode would jam the guidance systems of others nearby, and create unpredictable changes in wind patterns, throwing the later missiles off course. An attack staggered over several hours to avoid fratricide would give the U.S. ample time to respond.

Fratricide aside, many critics doubt the possibility of guiding any missile accurately enough to destroy a reinforced silo thousands of miles away. The strength of the earth's gravitation, for example, varies slightly from point to point. An error in calculating the strength of gravitation along a missile's path by as much as three parts in a million (about the amount of gravitation you feel from the moon) would lead to missing the target by several hundred feet and failing to blow up the hardened silo. Shifting winds and variations in the earth's magnetic field are also likely to throw a missile off course by hundreds, if not thousands, of feet.[4]

The U.S. has learned to compensate for these factors on its missile test range in the Pacific, where the results of many test firings have been analyzed. Neither the U.S. nor the U.S.S.R., however, has ever had the opportunity to test missiles fired over the North Pole and then over thousands of miles of foreign territory—the route which would be taken in an actual war. Under these conditions, the chances are quite remote that either side could succeed in a first strike that knocked out almost all the other side's silos.

Thus our mutual destruction is assured by land-based missiles as well as by submarines. The often-cited statistic that the Russians have more and heavier land-based missiles is not of any great significance. We have many more submarine-based weapons then they do. Above all, both sides have more than enough, both on land and underwater.

However thin its basis in reality, the supposed threat of a Soviet first strike is being used to justify a chilling change in U.S. military planning. Top administration officials no longer seem to think that U.S. use of nuclear weapons is quite as unthinkable as it used to be. Vice President George Bush has asserted that a "limited nuclear war" is winnable. Secretary of State Alexander Haig has claimed that there are worse things than nuclear war, and managed to terrify millions of people on both sides of the Atlantic by casually mentioning the possibility of exploding a nuclear "warning shot" over Europe if conventional war breaks out.

Officials at a slightly lower level are even more explicit. T.K. Jones, deputy undersecretary of defense for strategic and nuclear forces, believes it would take only two to four years for the United States to fully recover from an all-out nuclear attack. The Federal Emergency Management Agency, which is in charge of civil defense, cheerfully claims, "Even under the worst circumstances imaginable there would be no danger of a repetition of the bubonic plague that devastated Europe in the mid-14th century." The agency recommends that you build a "pre-planned snack bar shelter" in your basement, which can double as an entertainment center before and, they hope, after the attack.

Planning for the United States after the apocalypse has reached impressive levels of detail. The Postal Service has prepared Emergency Change of Address Cards (Form 809) for use following a nuclear attack. The Treasury Department warns banks to expect the bond market to be temporarily depressed. The IRS plans to forgive all back taxes, since its computerized records would presumably be destroyed by radiation. One weak spot is the Public Health Service, which apparently has not updated its plan for "sanitary aspects of disposal of the dead" since 1956. (That 1956 plan recommended digging large ditches.) Through it all, civil defense director William Chipman offers his confidence that the survivors "would in all probability rise to the occasion and restore some kind of a country that would fairly be called the post-attack United States. . . . As I say, ants will eventually build another anthill."[5]

Ants, however, are distinctly more likely to survive than human beings, as insects have proved able to withstand doses of radioactivity that are lethal to mammals. In short, it appears that a war that could mean the end of human life on earth is becoming a live option for Ronald Reagan's Pentagon planners. Since the United States already has the invulnerable capability to fight that final war many times over, there is no sensible argument for more nuclear weapons—and quite a compelling case for disarmament.

The CIA's Soviet Budgets

In conventional, non-nuclear forces, the U.S. position is also secure. The Soviet armed forces do have many more active duty personnel, but large numbers are occupied with jobs done by civilians in the U.S., with internal security or with defending the border with China. The U.S. has felt no comparable need to put hundreds of thousands of soldiers along the Canadian or Mexican border. As a result the two superpowers have approximately equal numbers of troops available for the titanic Central European battle which looms so large in the minds of our military planners. In addition, our European allies have much larger armies than theirs do. Total NATO troops available for war in Europe well outnumber their Warsaw Pact counterparts.[6]

The Soviet lead in conventional military hardware also looks much less ominous on close inspection. They have a larger number of ships, but we have a greater tonnage of ships and more naval firepower. They have more tanks, but the last Middle East war showed tanks to be increasingly vulnerable to new "smart" (computer-guided) anti-tank weapons, an area in which we are years ahead. The Soviet military machine is quite capable of invading a small country like Afghanistan, though not able to pacify it; there is no evidence that it threatens the United States or Western Europe.

Much has been made of the supposed Soviet military buildup of recent years. The media frequently reports that Soviet arms spending doubled in the 1970s; Ronald Reagan says that the U.S.S.R. outspent us by $300 billion in that decade. These claims rest on two separate statistics produced by the CIA. Both claims contain serious flaws.

If you examine the CIA's periodic estimates of military spending as a percentage of Soviet GNP, you will indeed find that the estimates roughly doubled during the 1970s. If you examine them even more closely, you will find that the doubling of the figures took place overnight during 1976. The CIA abruptly decided, apparently based on information supplied by a Soviet defector, that the prices charged by Soviet weapons factories were much higher than previously believed. Nothing was changed about the estimates of the numbers of tanks, missiles, or ships being produced; only the estimated fraction of Soviet national income spent on weapons was raised. In part the higher estimates reflected the CIA's conclusion that Soviet weapons factories were much less efficient than previously believed, and therefore had to charge higher prices—hardly evidence of an increased threat to the West.

The change that took place in 1976, it should be emphasized, was a change in U.S. knowledge (or perhaps guesses), not in Soviet reality. The CIA now believes Soviet weapons production has been inefficient all along, and hence the fraction of Soviet GNP spent on weapons has always been rather high. The pre-1976 estimates have been thrown out, and the recalculated estimates for earlier years do not show any alarming growth. A 1980 CIA report said that Soviet military spending, corrected for inflation, increased by an annual average of only 3% in the 1970s.[7] Thus the often-cited doubling of Soviet military spending rests solely on a misunderstanding of the changes in CIA estimates.

Misleading as the CIA's changing estimates of Soviet budgets have been, their comparisons of Soviet and U.S. spending have been even worse. The $300 billion by which the U.S.S.R. outspent us in the last decade is purely a figment of the CIA's statistical imagination.

There are some genuine problems in comparing Soviet and U.S. budgets. Merely converting rubles to dollars at the current exchange rate may be misleading because the patterns of prices are so different. For example, comparisons of consumer incomes are hard to interpret because Soviet cars and other consumer goods are extremely expensive by U.S. standards, while medical care is free and housing and mass transit are very cheap. Similar problems hamper the comparison of military budgets.

Faced with this statistical difficulty, the CIA arbitrarily employs a method which is sure to exaggerate Soviet spending. The CIA catalogues all the labor and equipment used by the Soviet military, and then calculates how much it would cost to buy the same things in the U.S. Soviet draftees are assumed to be receiving U.S. volunteer army pay rates; Soviet tanks are assumed to cost whatever the Pentagon is paying for tanks; and so on.[8]

One ludicrous effect of this approach is that every pay raise for U.S. soldiers raises the Soviet military budget. In fact, theirs is a more labor-intensive military apparatus than ours; soldiers' pay makes up a larger fraction of the military budget in the Soviet Union than in the United States. So every U.S.

pay raise causes a proportionally greater increase in their budget than in ours, widening the supposed gap in military spending. Reagan has promised to increase U.S. soldiers' pay, thereby also ensuring that the Soviet lead in military spending will continue to exist in the CIA figures.

Another problem with the CIA calculation is that, even on its own terms, it only works as long as you forget about Europe. Again, our Western European allies have much larger military budgets than the Soviet Union's Eastern European ones. Even using the CIA method of calculation, total NATO military spending is slightly greater than total Warsaw Pact spending.[9]

A more believable estimate, from the Stockholm International Peace Research Institute, found the two superpowers about equal in arms spending before the Reagan buildup.[10] That estimate would imply that NATO as a whole was substantially outspending the Warsaw Pact.

The Best-Made Planes. . . .

In short, a good Soviet threat is hard to find. Yet anti-Soviet rhetoric has justified the colossal, and now rapidly growing, expense of our military establishment, the unparalleled repository of the waste which Ronald Reagan promised to eliminate from federal government. Some of it would be amusing, if it wasn't our money; the Navy buys shipboard tape recorders which cost 47 times as much as equivalent civilian models.[11]

Or there is the story of the Army's new armored personnel carrier, once scheduled to be delivered by 1965. Fifteen years and many expensive modifications later, a prototype of this allegedly amphibious Infantry Fighting Vehicle (IFV) was unveiled. The *Wall Street Journal* described the scene:

> In the summer of 1980, the cavalry proudly rolled out its version of the IFV for testing in front of Maj. Gen. Louis Wagner, other dignitaries and a local television crew at Fort Knox. It drove into the Ohio River and promptly sank. Something was wrong with a latch related to a

rubberized nylon collar that should allow the vehicle to float.

The embarrassment was nothing compared to the uproar the following December when it was reported that the total cost of the IFV program had risen from $7.4 billion to more than $13 billion in one year.

Now renamed the Bradley Fighting Vehicle, it is currently scheduled to roll, or perhaps float, into active duty in 1983.[12]

To see money being wasted in truly grand style, however, you have to look at bigger weapons programs—like the latest Air Force fighter planes. "Tactical Air" squadrons, those planes not intended for nuclear assault on the Soviet Union, were one of the military growth areas of the late 1970s, in some years swallowing as much as a quarter of the entire Pentagon budget. That money was spent on the latest, most complex and most expensive planes, like the F-15, at $30 million each—planes whose great cost is due to exotic capabilities which are almost certain to never be used.

One of the quickest ways to make a plane expensive is to demand that it go faster. A plane designed to fly above twice the speed of sound (Mach 2) cannot be made out of anything as common as aluminum. Materials such as titanium, stainless steel and beryllium, none of them cheap, are required for the airframe. The engines also must be bigger and more complex, and be made of more costly materials.

But, as one of the most important Pentagon leaks of recent years revealed, in actual wars pilots do not fly at these speeds. In the Vietnam war, U.S. pilots flew more than 100,000 flights in planes capable of exceeding Mach 2. Only one instance of a few seconds above Mach 1.6 was ever recorded. Only a total of a few minutes of flight time even reached Mach 1.4. Moreover, supersonic flight burns fuel at an exorbitant rate. The one flight which reached Mach 1.6 ran out of fuel; the pilots bailed out over North Vietnam and were captured.

Aside from running out of fuel, another reason why fighter planes are not flown faster is that pilots have to identify enemy planes visually before firing at them. The theoretical solution has been to install complex electronic systems to identify and target planes that are not yet in sight. These systems work well in one-on-one simulations, but have no way of distinguishing friendly from enemy planes in crowded, chaotic skies with many blips crossing each other on radar screens. In practice pilots will likely continue to go slow enough and get close enough to see what they are shooting at.

The new electronic systems have been a tremendous success, however, at eating up money. Each F-15 has 45 separate computer circuits which can, and often do, break down and need replacement. Even the computers used in the repair shop to locate the F-15's problems have their own frequent breakdowns, and the Air Force has been unable to recruit and retain enough computer technicians to make the system run smoothly. A 1980 Defense Department memo showed the average F-15 was ready to fly only 56% of the time, and needed 34 hours of maintenance per flight. Another new plane, the F-111D, was ready to fly 34% of the time and required 98 maintenance hours per flight.[13]

Supersonic flight, while it may help, is not a prerequisite for creating such defects. Similar problems have shown up in the Army's new M-1 Abrams tank, costing $2.7 million apiece. Loaded with complex new systems never before installed in a tank, the M-1 appears to have become useless in any actual battle. It has a breakdown requiring 30 minutes or more to fix, on average, every 43 miles. It gets less than 1400 *feet* to a gallon of gas, so it must be accompanied by a fuel truck. Its transmission is too fragile to allow it to dig itself into fortified positions, as earlier tanks did, so it must also be accompanied by a specialized bulldozer. Its gun wobbles in cold weather, its hydraulic fluid is extremely flammable, its turbine engine is an easier target for heat-seeking missiles than earlier diesel engines, its side, top and rear armor is thinner than on earlier tanks, and on and on. The U.S. M-60 tank which it will replace did much better by most of these standards, as do current Soviet tanks.[14]

A similar story could be told about other high-technology, high-priced weapons. There is no plausible use for some of the most expensive new toys at the Pentagon, just as there is no real military spending gap between the U.S. and the U.S.S.R., and no credible threat of a nuclear first strike or a European invasion by either side against the other.

How Much Is Enough?

Much of our defense spending, in other words, is not really of any use in defending us. How much—or how little—do we need? The answer will depend on how far we can go in reducing international tensions and conflicts. Suppose, then, we examine the worst possible case. If all disarmament negotiations continue to fail, if world tensions cannot be reduced, how much would we have to spend to defend ourselves and our allies?

This worst-case scenario has been examined in detail by the Boston Study Group, a liberal academic group concerned with military issues. Assuming all present defensive obligations would continue to be met, they proposed "that the U.S. buy as much force as it needs but not more, that it prepare prudently for military contingencies but not overprepare." After a painstaking weapon-by-weapon, program-by-program review of Defense Department spending, they concluded that to defend the U.S., Western Europe, Israel and Japan, and to maintain an invulnerable nuclear deterrent, we needed only $73 billion in 1978, or about $110 billion in 1982 dollars—roughly 60% of the 1982 military budget, or well under half the amount that Reagan is shooting for in 1984 and beyond.[15]

Regardless of what the Soviet Union or other countries do, therefore, we could cut military spending to $110 billion without impairing anyone's security. This would do more than save us a lot of money. As the Boston Study Group noted, a unilateral U.S. reduction to the levels they proposed would be a dramatic signal of our peaceful intentions, and might lead to successful arms control talks and further reductions.

Back in the real world, the Pentagon is spending an estimated $188 billion in 1982, and much more in later years. The excess military spending, above the Boston Study Group's worst-case estimate of real need, is already $78 billion a year, soon to be much higher—far greater than the cuts in the civilian budget.

Why are we spending so much more than, by any standard, we need for defense? If the Pentagon were just another federal agency, David Stockman would have been unleashed on it by now. It was a task he once looked forward to. As he put it, "Hell, I think there's a kind of swamp of $10 to $20 to $30 billion worth of waste that can be ferreted out if you really push hard." (For once in his life, Stockman may have been guilty of being too lenient, having identified much less waste than the Boston Study Group was able to.)

But the Pentagon is not just another agency, and Stockman has not been allowed to touch it. Despite decades of anticommunist rhetoric, defense is not really the major goal of the Defense Department. The swollen military budget plays important roles in our political economy, both in relation to the rest of the world and in domestic life.

Winning One For the Gipper

One goal of military spending beyond our defensive needs is to regain the power we once had to dominate smaller nations. Before the Vietnam war the U.S. was able to intervene at will in most underdeveloped countries. Alliances, military aid, occasional CIA coups, even visits from the Marines were used to keep friendly governments in power throughout the "Free World." It was not a world of political freedom that we were defending; the rulers of Indonesia, Brazil and other Free World stalwarts (like our allies in El Salvador and Guatemala today) were in the habit of torturing and killing any visible opposition. But it was a world in which multinational corporations were free to come and go as they pleased, an alliance for profits if not always for progress.

Overseas activity has proved profitable indeed for U.S. business. The share of corporate profits coming from foreign investment has mounted steadily since World War II, reaching 24% by 1980.[16] While more than half of this comes from Europe and Canada, the U.S. corporate stake in the Third World is also substantial. U.S. companies depend on foreign oil and other raw materials, on foreign markets for their exports and on the growing opportunities to invest in low-wage manufacturing abroad.

In the early 1970s U.S. control of this economic empire was dealt a disastrous double blow. Defeat in Indochina revealed the limits of military intervention, while the rise of OPEC weakened U.S. control over the most important foreign resource. Saving "our" oil in particular, and our access to Third World economies in general, seemed to require a new strategy.

For a few years the Pentagon and the State Department leaned toward the development of regional policemen, or "sub-imperial powers," as they were sometimes called. The U.S. would send military aid to Brazil, allowing the Brazilian military to be the guardians of South America. Or, in the most important, best-armed case, massive aid to the Shah of Iran would surely allow him to keep the Middle East under control. . . .

The downfall of the Shah in early 1979 ended the brief era of reliance on other countries to police the Third World for us. Not that regional allies became irrelevant; U.S. military aid and weapons sales to Turkey, Egypt, Saudi Arabia and Pakistan increased after the "loss" of Iran. But more important was the massive propaganda campaign for a renewed U.S. military buildup. Then, a year later, when the Soviet Union invaded Afghanistan—the kind of event that U.S. right wingers had spent thirty years breathlessly waiting for—the floodgates of the new militarism were pushed wide open.

Seeing no other military option, the Pentagon has returned to a post-Shah policy remarkably like pre-Vietnam policy; once again, the best defense is a strong offense. Maybe we can win the next one for the Gipper. The Marines appear to be searching for their roots; they could well be returning to Central America, just south of the halls of Montezuma, or to Libya, formerly known as the shores of Tripoli.

Thus several chunks of Reagan's military spending are aimed at improving our ability to attack Third World countries that displease us. The Rapid Deployment Force is supposed to be able to put 24,000 troops and their weapons in the Persian Gulf area, or almost anywhere else in the world, on two weeks' notice. Its expenses for such items as desert fighting gear and Indian Ocean bases are of little relevance to defending the United States.

The Navy's expansion from 450 to 600 ships, one of Reagan's most expensive plans for the 1980s, is also aimed at Third World intervention. The Soviet Union and its allies have almost no warm-water ocean ports, and are far behind us in naval tonnage and firepower. Moreover, our lead is increasing.

Even a 1981 Pentagon puff piece, "Soviet Military Power," admitted that we had 42 major surface warships under construction to the Soviet Union's 12.[17] There is no credible Soviet naval threat at which our new ships are aimed.

The large size of many of our ships, paradoxically, constitutes further evidence that they are intended to intimidate poorly-armed Third World nations. Our biggest ships are so expensive that they can only be used against countries that have no chance of sinking them. Even the Pentagon, with its privileged access to the nation's treasury, cannot afford to have a destroyer (costing up to $1 billion) or a nuclear-powered aircraft carrier ($3 billion) sunk by one of the new computer-guided anti-ship missiles.

These "smart" anti-ship weapons give a tremendous economic advantage to the defense. In the 1967 war Egypt used one of the earliest such weapons, a missile developed by the Soviet Union in the 1950s, to sink an Israeli destroyer from miles away. The destroyer cost $150 million; the missile that sank it cost $20,000. Because the missile had a range of 20 miles, it could be launched from a small patrol boat outside the reach of the destroyer's guns. Since then smart anti-ship weapons have been used successfully by both Israel and Egypt, and by India against Pakistan in the 1971 clash. The newest missiles have much more advanced guidance systems, and longer ranges, than the one Egypt used in 1967.[18]

Our biggest-ticket items of all, the nuclear-powered aircraft carriers, are so immense—they have six-acre flight decks—as to present easy targets for an attack. Aircraft carriers were developed in an era when ships could not reliably be sunk at such long distances; today their use is limited to being kept far offshore and far away from enemy ships, or more likely, being used against countries which do not yet have modern anti-ship weapons.

One major savings proposed by the Boston Study Group is a reduction from 13 to 3 nuclear aircraft carriers. Each one taken out of service saves roughly $200 million annually, the operating costs of a carrier and its accompanying ships. In addition, the accompanying ships could be reassigned to other uses, reducing the number of new vessels the Navy plans to build. Instead the Reagan administration has decided to build two more giant carriers, committing us to spending $12 billion ($3 billion for each carrier, and about that much again for accompanying ships) during the 1980s. Meanwhile, computers are getting smaller, cheaper and more powerful all the time, and it is reasonable to expect that computer-guided anti-ship missiles will do the same. When carriers number 14 and 15 hit the water in 1991 or thereafter, how far will anti-ship weaponry have progressed?

As they say in Washington, throwing money at problems does not always solve them. Our pre-Vietnam ability to control other countries will not be restored at the sight of a fourteenth or fifteenth aircraft carrier. Our overwhelming military superiority did not hasten the return of U.S. hostages from Iran in 1980. Nor are we really likely to invade an oil-producing country and seize its oilfields; a handful of people opposing our invasion could quickly sabotage wells and pipelines in ways that would take years to repair.

Shooting down a few Libyan planes, as we did in 1981, may remind other countries that we are armed and dangerous, and make them think twice about speaking crossly to us. It will undoubtedly strengthen our hand in some minor conflicts. But that is not the same as being able to win the next Vietnam-style war or to save the next dictator who, like the Shah, is threatened by his own people.

The War at Home

> What do we care whether they (Lockheed) perform? We are guaranteeing them basically a $250 million loan. What for? . . . . so they can provide employment for 31,000 people throughout the country at a time when we desperately need that type of employment. . . .
> —Former Treasury Secretary
> John Connally, 1971[19]

In the realm of actual foreign events much of our armed forces, and of our military spending, must be judged redundant for defense and problematical for offense. Yet in another theater of conflict, closer to home, there is a proven value to titanium airplanes, $3 billion aircraft carriers and MX missiles wherever they are finally based. Military spending has played an important role in the post-World War II domestic economy, and seems destined to play an even larger role under Reagan.

One of the lessons of the Great Depression of the 1930s was that private business does not, on its own, reliably provide anything close to full employment. The economist John Maynard Keynes became famous for proposing a solution to massive unemployment—deficit spending by the government—and for developing an economic theory which explained why it worked. Less well known is Keynes' grudging awareness of the way in which his ideas would be carried out.

> It is, it seems, politically impossible for a capitalistic democracy to organize expenditure on the scale necessary to make the grand experiment which would prove my case—except in war conditions.[20]

Events proved Keynes' cynicism partially correct. The official unemployment rate remained above 14% throughout the 1930s; it was World War II, not the New Deal or the impact of Keynesian ideas, which ended the depression. After the war, a brief period of lowered arms spending in the late 1940s ran into the recession of 1949–50, raising fears of renewed depression; that recession was ended by the Korean War, which again boosted the military budget. After the Korean War, the politics of the Cold War kept military spending far above prewar levels. Between the end of the Korean War and the election of Ronald Reagan, the Pentagon's budget roughly kept up with inflation (leaving aside the peak years of fighting in Vietnam).

As noted in Chapter 1, other areas of government grew more rapidly. By the late 1970s the military absorbed "only" about one-fourth of federal spending, or one-seventh of federal, state and local spending combined. Still, the Pentagon was the nation's largest employment agency, with 3% of the labor force on its payroll—2% in uniform, 1% in civilian jobs at the Defense Department. In addition, military purchases of goods and services from private contractors accounted for about another 3% of the gross national product.[21] So the Pentagon and its suppliers directly employed something like 6% of us, even at the military's lowest point of relative importance in the last thirty years.

Viewed as insurance against depressions, the role of the military is even larger. In a situation like the 1930s, a program that suddenly provided direct employment for 6% of the labor force would cause a surge in consumer spending. Formerly unemployed people, receiving paychecks from the Pentagon or from Lockheed, would go out and spend more money; industries making consumer goods would then hire more workers, who in turn would spend more money, and so on. Ultimately, direct employment for 6% of the labor force would create indirect employment for roughly another 6%. Therefore, if the alternative was sinking into depression, the military budget of the late 1970s was responsible, directly and indirectly, for about 12% of all employment.

(Notice that this figure is crucially dependent on what the alternative was. If the alternative was a program providing full employment in non-military activities, then the Pentagon was simply taking 6% of the labor force away from peaceful pursuits, not increasing total employment at all.)

Critics have often argued that military spending provides fewer jobs and less technological progress than other programs would. For instance, one study found that transferring 30% of the Pentagon budget to education, health, welfare and environmental programs would increase both output and employment by 2%. Seymour Melman and others have suggested that the concentration of the nation's research and development effort on weapons industries is responsible for the lack of productivity growth in civilian manufacturing over the last decade.[22] As far as most of us are concerned, such statements are certainly true; it is easy to imagine alternative programs that, for the same amount of money, could produce more jobs and technological progress than the Pentagon does. Equally important, those alternatives would pose less of a threat to human life than the military does.

But from the point of view of business, military spending is more attractive than most other government programs. Some alternatives would compete with private industry; more mass transit or public housing would not help the auto or private housing industries. Social welfare spending, of course, weakens the "work incentives" so popular with employers.

The Pentagon does none of this, but instead creates new industries, such as aerospace, and profitable sidelines for many other manufacturers. As Chrysler sank ever deeper into the red in recent years, its most reliable source of profits was the division that produced those fancy, non-functional M-1 tanks. (By early 1982, however, Chrysler had to sell its tank division in the endless quest for cash to cover its auto losses.) Though other programs might theoretically do even better, new technologies in electronics have spun off from military procurement; the computer wizardry in the latest weapons can stimulate profits and technological change, whether or not it is of conceivable use in combat.

Solid figures are hard to find, but it appears reasonable to guess that military contracts accounted for 8% or more of total corporate profits, even at the relative low point of the late 1970s.[23] For the leading defense contractors, of course, Pentagon-sponsored profits were much more important. It is not surprising that these firms have joined with the top brass of the Armed Forces to form a powerful, successful lobby for the continuation and expansion of their favorite weapons programs.

The military is not the only program to offer many of these advantages to businessmen. Shooting expensive rockets into outer space meets most of the same criteria quite nicely, even guaranteeing profits to some of the same corporations, and has indeed been tried at times. No way has been found, however, to attach the same moral urgency to improvements in our knowledge of astronomy as to safeguards against the supposed Soviet threat. Thus space exploration, a much smaller program to begin with, has won only very modest budget increases under Reagan. The only NASA program that enjoys Pentagon-style affluence is the space shuttle, prized for its ability to launch military satellites.

Whether conservatives realize it or not (some do and some don't), the moral imperative they attach to military spending is essential to their economic program. It allows them to prattle on about the virtues of reducing the role of the government without having to carry it out across the board. Theory to the contrary, boosts in one major area of public spending remain legitimate, almost sacred, in their eyes.

The very size of the military budgets scheduled for the mid-1980s indicates that Reagan's top advisors know supply-side economics will not work. If it were to work, if the tax cut were sufficient to send production and employment soaring, then military and civilian industry would soon be competing for limited supplies of investment funds and productive facilities. The president's economic advisors, still publicly committed to forecasts of a rosy recovery, have begun to predict that some civilian investments will have to be postponed or cancelled in the next few years to accommodate the military boom.[24]

It is more likely, however, that supply-side theory will continue to fail. If, as also seems likely, the government sticks to its policy of fighting inflation through tight money and high interest rates, then the Reagan recession may well drag on for a while, breaking one record after another to establish itself as the worst since the 1930s. In this case the upsurge in weapons spending will seem to make a certain kind of economic sense. Like the Great Depression, the near-great slump of the early 1980s may be ended only by preparation for war. In this scenario, unlike the glowing official predictions, an internal logic can be found in Reaganomics. Perhaps the Pentagon budget was designed as a safety net to catch falling economic advisors.

There is a more immediate ulterior motive, as well, for the massive military effort. If we "need" both a big tax cut and a big boost in our defenses, then it is easy to prove that, even allowing moderately large deficits, we cannot afford to continue our past levels of civilian government spending. For some this may be a conclusion reached reluctantly; for others it is a welcome new weapon in the longstanding battle against social reforms and income redistribution. The specifics of the Reagan military agenda are no more important in budgetary politics than on the battlefield—what matters is that the total is so large as to ensure that something else has got to go.

CHAPTER 5

Chopping Through
the Net

*We are interested in curtailing weak claims rather
than weak clients.*

—David Stockman

One of the weak claims—or is it a weak client?—is the rat
control program in New York City. In the late 1960s, when
federal spending for urban rodent control began, 750 rat bites
were reported annually in the Big Apple. More recently the
number of bites has fallen to close to 200. However, the 1982
federal budget lumps the $13.5 million formerly spent on ro-
dent control ($1.5 million of it in New York City) together
with many other preventive health services, and cuts the funding for the entire group of programs 17% below the level authorized when Reagan took office.[1]

The most notorious of all weak claims on the public treasury, the scapegoats everyone loves to hate, are able-bodied
men receiving welfare checks. One of those men is Amos Coalburn, a 42-year-old Milwaukee truckdriver who has been unemployed since his last employer went out of business, and

now collects general assistance. When blizzards buried Milwaukee in January 1982, Coalburn told local officials he had been on welfare "too long" and applied for a job operating the city's heavy snow-removal equipment. The city did not hire him, but by February Coalburn was at work removing snow—with a shovel, and without a paycheck. Under the county's new workfare program he was forced to work off his welfare check at $3.50 an hour. "They wouldn't hire me before and now they turn around and tell me I have to work for nothing," said Coalburn, shaking his head.[2] Reagan's 1983 budget would make workfare programs mandatory in all states.

> None of us really understands what's going on with all these numbers . . . we were doing that whole budget-cutting exercise so frenetically. In other words, you were juggling details, pushing people, and going from one session to another, trying to cut housing programs here and rural electric there, and we were doing it so fast, we didn't know where we were ending up for sure. . . .
>
> —David Stockman

Sadly enough, it is all too clear where the budget-cutters are ending up. With the tax cut and the military buildup in place, with mushrooming interest payments on the national debt, with a temporary truce declared in efforts to slash basic services for the elderly, almost everything else in the budget is scheduled for devastation.

A simple test will serve to identify the favored sections of the budget, and will reveal much about the administration's real priorities. In Reagan's proposed 1983 budget, which items are scheduled to grow faster than inflation? Only seven programs pass this test, though they swallow the lion's share of the budget; they are the first seven entries in Table 2.

There is the military, of course, with actual spending projected to grow 18% from 1982 to 1983, and authorization for future spending (not shown in the table) growing even faster. There are the smaller allocations for foreign affairs, and for space and scientific research, growing at more modest rates, but still growing. Interest payments on the national debt are

TABLE 2: THE FEDERAL BUDGET, 1981-83
(in billions of dollars)

	1981 actual	1982 estimated	1983 proposed
TOTAL*	657	728	761
Military	160	188	221
Foreign affairs	11	11	12
Space, science	6	7	8
Interest**	68	83	96
Major programs for the elderly:			
Social Security	138	155	174
Medicare	39	46	51
Federal employee pensions	18	19	21
SUBTOTAL: ALL OTHER SPENDING	233	234	205
Training, employment (includes CETA)	9	5	3
Unemployment compensation	20	25	23
Food stamps, child nutrition	16	16	14
AFDC	9	8	6
Medicaid	17	18	17
Housing assistance	7	8	9
Education	15	15	13
Other health (includes OSHA)	10	10	10
Other social services and benefits	25	26	21
Energy, resources, environment*	24	22	17
Transportation	23	21	20
Veterans programs	23	24	24
Commerce, development, revenue-sharing	20	18	16
Agriculture	6	9	4
General government, law enforcement	10	10	10
Undistributed offsetting receipts***	−17	−15	−27

All figures are fiscal year (October 1–September 30) outlay totals, rounded to the nearest billion; details may not add to totals due to rounding.

*—Administration figures include the cost of the strategic petroleum reserve for 1981, but arbitrarily exclude it in 1982 and 1983. Here it is included for all years, adding $3 billion to administration figures for 1982 and 1983.

**—Total interest paid minus interest received by federal trust funds.

***—Several minor sources of funds are always listed this way, as "negative expenditures" in the budget. The figures presented here exclude interest received by federal trust funds. The largest undistributed offsetting receipt is income from Outer Continental Shelf oil and gas wells, projected to more than double in 1983.

Source: *Budget of the United States Government, Fiscal Year 1983.*

being pushed upward both by Reagan's huge deficits, increasing the need for new borrowing, and by high interest rates.

The only areas of social spending where projected growth beats inflation are the three major programs for the elderly: Social Security, Medicare, and federal employee pensions. (On the apparent growth in housing funds, see page 88). It is not for lack of desire to cut that elderly services are being spared—Reagan has tried, but so far failed, to pare them down. In 1981 the administration suffered its first major defeat when it tackled the issue of Social Security cuts, winning only a fraction of what it asked for and encountering massive popular opposition to any further reduction in benefits. The attack on Social Security is not over (more on this below), but does appear to have been postponed until after the 1982 elections; the 1983 budget proposals, released in early 1982, call for no new cuts.[3]

Having retreated for the time being on Social Security, the budget-cutters are trying a bit of sniping at Medicare instead. Medical care for the elderly and the disabled escaped unscathed in Reagan's first budget; for 1983 the administration wants to reduce payments to hospitals by 2%, to increase the Medicare deductible paid by the patient (now $75) along with inflation, and to charge 5% payment for formerly free home health care services.[4] Like the attempt to cut Social Security a year earlier, these changes would save the government very little money. As shown in Table 2, Medicare costs would continue to rise in 1983 even with the changes. If successful, however, reductions in either Medicare or Social Security could begin to accustom the public to the idea of cuts in once-sacred retirement programs—paving the way for much deeper cuts to come.

Sniping at Medicare aside, Reagan appears to have accepted that, at least through the 1983 budget, it is politically impossible to make significant cuts in elderly services. These programs, along with the military, foreign affairs, space exploration, and interest on the debt, consume the bulk of the budget: about two-thirds in 1981 and 1982, and closer to three-quarters in the 1983 proposals.

The amount left for *all other* federal programs was $233 billion in 1981. In 1982, the year of Reagan's first budget, the corresponding amount was almost identical, $234 billion.[5] However, the cost of maintaining 1981 levels of services was much greater, both because of inflation and because of the increased need for benefits like unemployment compensation and food stamps during a recession. The roughly constant budget total for all other programs in 1982 thus implies a cut in services.

Merely adjusting the 1982 total for all other programs to keep up with inflation would require a $14 billion increase for 1983.[5] Instead, Reagan proposes a $29 billion decrease, to $205 billion—in other words, $43 billion less than would be needed to keep up with inflation.

Cut, Cut, Cut

> Do you have any idea what $40 billion means? It means I've got to cut the highway program. It means I've got to cut milk-price supports. And Social Security student benefits. And education and student loans. And manpower training and housing. It means I've got to shut down the synfuels program and a lot of other programs.
>
> —David Stockman

Despite the air of frenzied slashing in every direction, a definite pattern can be seen in Reagan's budget cuts, both those enacted for 1982 and those proposed for 1983. The very area the administration claims to be protecting, the "essential safety net" of programs for the "truly needy," in fact bears the brunt of the attack. Basic urban services and environmental programs are being cut as well, while functions valued by business are continuing to thrive. The "New Federalism" proposals and the move toward block grants, cloaked in rhetoric about states' rights and decentralization, are actually attempts to shift the responsibility for painful cutbacks away from Washington and onto state and local governments.[6]

There is no mistaking the fact: the cutbacks are painful. Just ask someone like Danny Salb. A teenager in a welfare family in Connecticut, Danny had been angry and frustrated in eighth grade. "I was flunking everything," he recalled. Then he got a part-time CETA (Comprehensive Employment and

Training Act) job at a dog pound, fell in love with the animals, and decided to become a veterinarian. After a few weeks, a teacher noted, "Danny felt better about himself." His grades improved, and he used the money he earned on his job to help his mother buy groceries and to buy clothes for himself.

In the fall of 1981, as Danny Salb was beginning ninth grade, he and more than 300,000 other CETA employees were laid off by Ronald Reagan. "I was pretty upset," said Danny. His mother said he had counted on spending his income to buy the shoes he needed for the winter.[7]

CETA was the 1970s version of public works, the federal government's admission that jobs had to be created for some of the people who could not find work in the private sector. At its peak in 1977–78 CETA's main public service employment program funded three-quarters of a million jobs, enough to knock almost a full percentage point off the unemployment rate. By the end of the Carter administration CETA had shrunk to about half that size; in Reagan's first budget CETA was, as David Stockman likes to say, "zeroed out"—abolished. The Job Corps and other training programs have been slashed as well, leading to a projected cut in federal spending on employment and training from $9 billion in 1981 to $3 billion in 1983.

The Reagan administration has not only laid off people. It has also made life harder for those who are unemployed. Trade adjustment assistance (TAA) used to provide a full year of unemployment benefits to people who lost their jobs due to imports. Half a million workers, most of them laid off by the auto industry and its suppliers, were receiving TAA when Ronald Reagan came to power. The 1982 budget cut more than half the funds for TAA, and the 1983 proposals would finish off all traces of TAA except a tiny retraining program.

In the days before Reagan it was possible to collect unemployment benefits on leaving the armed forces, and 140,000 ex-soldiers were doing so in 1981. Now there is a new, one-word alternative: re-enlist. Benefits are being denied to anyone eligible for re-enlistment, and to anyone receiving a bad conduct discharge. Unless the Pentagon decides to reduce its forces and begins involuntary layoffs, the only people eligible for unemployment benefits on leaving the military are those disabled while in service. Again, this change was largely carried out in 1982, and would be completed in the 1983 proposals.

Moreover, Reagan's 1982 budget made unemployment compensation stingier all around. A new regulation required that people out of work 13 weeks or longer had to take any job offering as much as half their former pay, or lose benefits. And changes in the complex regulations governing extended benefits turned out to disqualify almost everyone from receiving those benefits, just as massive layoffs got underway in late 1981.

The extension of unemployment compensation from the usual 26 weeks to 39 weeks used to be automatically "triggered" on by increases in the national unemployment rate. Perhaps as a preview of the New Federalism, Reagan did away with the national trigger, leaving only a choice of two difficult criteria which must be met state by state. With these criteria the administration was able to halt extended benefits even in Michigan, a state suffering depression-level unemployment due to the auto slump, for three months in the winter of 1981–82.

Under the fiscal 1982 budget rules, a state could only pay extended benefits when the insured unemployment rate (IUR)—the percentage of the state labor force collecting their first 26 weeks of unemployment checks—rose high enough. Either the IUR had to exceed 5%, or the IUR had to be *both* over 4% *and* over 120% of its level a year earlier. Although Michigan had very high unemployment throughout 1981, many of the state's jobless workers had been laid off for more than 26 weeks, and thus no longer showed up in the IUR. In early November 1981 the state IUR briefly dipped to 4.93%, failing the first criterion; and it was not 120% higher than the level in November 1980, so it failed the second criterion as well.

Under the Reagan rules, Michigan therefore lost all extended benefits for 13 weeks, even though the state IUR was back above 5% by late November and continued to climb thereafter. In December 1981, *no* Northeastern or Midwestern industrial state qualified for extended benefits, despite the deepening recession; only Alaska, Washington, Idaho, Alabama and Puerto Rico managed to pass one test or the other. By February 1982 Michigan's IUR was approaching 8%, and its total unemployment rate was pushing 14%, yet the state could not receive federal funds to resume extended benefits until March.[8] This from an administration that repeatedly promises to free us from the silly, cumbersome regulations of the past.

The extended benefit rules are not permanent, though. They are scheduled for improvement in 1983. The state triggers for extended benefits will be raised to an IUR of 6%, or over 5% and over 120% of the year-earlier level.

Grapes of Wrath

> Men who can graft the trees and make the seed fertile and big can find no way to let the hungry people eat their produce. Men who have created new fruits in the world cannot create a system whereby their fruits may be eaten. And the failure hangs over the State like a great sorrow. The works of the roots, of the vines, of the trees, must be destroyed to keep up the price, and this is the saddest, bitterest thing of all.
>
> —John Steinbeck[9]

The Grapes of Wrath, the classic saga of hunger and resistance in the Great Depression, sounds less like ancient history than it did a few years ago. As 1982 opens, small farms are going broke and being foreclosed in rising numbers. The federal government is buying surplus food, and paying farmers to produce less. At the same time, food stamps, school lunches and other programs that feed hungry people are being slashed.

Despite inflation, Reagan has lowered the eligibility ceiling for food stamps. The old upper limit for a family of four was an income of $14,000, the new limit is $11,000. Cost-of-living increases in benefits have been postponed, eligibility rules have been tightened, and the 1983 proposals, if enacted, will make food stamps still leaner. The administration wants to deduct 35¢ of benefits for every $1.00 increase in a recipient's income, rather than the present 30¢; it wants to lop off all fractions of a dollar, so that $50.95 in benefits becomes $50 instead of $51; and it hopes to cancel outright all benefits under $10 a month.

Other nutrition programs have also suffered. Food aid to Puerto Rico has been reduced. The supplemental food program for pregnant women, infants and children (WIC), which fended off attempted cuts in the 1982 budget, is under attack again for 1983. In the school lunch program, the proposed nutritional insight that ketchup is a vegetable was laughed out of court (with the result that subsidized school lunches must continue to include real vegetables); the less humorous cuts in eligibility for subsidized lunches, and in the dollar amount of subsidies, survived. For Massachusetts this meant that in Reagan's first year the average price of a school lunch rose from 50¢ to 85¢, and the number of lunches served in the schools fell by one-third.[10] To balance the budget, the poorest, hungriest people must be made to eat less—while the nation's farmers collapse under the weight of their embarrassingly unprofitable abundance.

Welfare Fraud

The most-maligned public program has been called on to sacrifice as well. Yet, popular stereotypes to the contrary, it is hard to solve very many economic problems at the expense of welfare. Aid to Families with Dependent Children (AFDC) accounts for only about 1% of the federal budget, as shown in Table 2. Ronald Reagan is not the first politician to perpetuate the fraud that welfare is becoming too expensive for the nation to afford. He has, however, acted on this misconception with particular ruthlessness.

Newly restrictive eligibility rules aim at cutting benefits and at throwing people off welfare entirely. Under the old rules welfare recipients who began to work only lost their benefits gradually as their incomes rose, to provide incentives for people to leave the welfare rolls. Under the Reagan rules benefits are lost much more quickly, as Kathleen Devlin found out.

Living in Wellfleet, Massachusetts with her two children, Devlin was on AFDC until October 1981. Then, having just started work as a bank teller, she was informed that her $500 monthly take-home pay made her ineligible for AFDC benefits under the new federal rules. But due to a bureaucratic error her welfare checks of almost $400 a month continued to arrive through the following January. She repeatedly asked her local welfare office if she was really entitled to the money; getting no definitive answer, she continued to cash and spend the checks. In February the Massachusetts Department of Public Welfare discovered its error and threatened to sue Devlin to recover the $1500 it had incorrectly sent her. "I have no money and no bank account," said Devlin. "And they want to take me to court. They make the mistake and they can still get the money back."[11]

Before the Reagan budgets took effect, more than one out of every four women on welfare already held a paying job—but one that paid so poorly that the woman was still eligible for AFDC. As these women face the loss of most or all of their benefits, some will likely decide that it is no longer worthwhile to keep working. Kathleen Devlin gets only about $100 a month more for going to work than she did for staying home on welfare; under the old rules her increase in income would have been at least twice as great, since she still would have qualified for partial benefits. Other welfare recipients, not yet working, will now decide that it is not worth the bother for such a small financial gain. This particular cutback, in other words, runs a risk of being self-defeating, since it could discourage people from leaving welfare and cost the government more, not less.

But as the carrot of monetary incentives to get off welfare is shrinking, the stick is getting bigger. Workfare programs, encouraged by Washington, were voluntarily adopted by most states in 1982 and will become mandatory in 1983. The most popular style of workfare requires welfare recipients to engage in mindless, endless job searches. In a "jobs club," for example, recipients are forced to put in 40 hours a week reading want ads, making telephone inquiries, writing resumes and going for interviews. This leads, if anywhere at all, to low-wage, dead-end, high-turnover positions—short-order cook, telephone salesperson, typist. Recipients are required to take the first job offer they get, regardless of location, pay, conditions, or child care availability.

By stressing rapid job placement, the program ignores the question of whether the job represents a long-term solution to welfare dependence. In a pilot program in Lowell, Massachusetts, more than 50 recipients complained that they had been forced to interrupt other training programs, some at the college level, which would have given them a chance to find permanent, skilled jobs. Instead, because of the low pay and high turnover in their "jobs club" placements, they may find themselves back on welfare in a few months.

A second version of workfare includes the Milwaukee program that sent Amos Coalburn out to shovel snow. Only women with children under six (in some states, only with children under two) are exempted; all other recipients are required to work off their grants in unpaid jobs, at a rate close to or equal to the minimum wage. The more children a welfare mother has, the larger her grant, and the more hours she must put in.

Either the jobs club or the snow-shovel style of workfare takes a mother away from her children for much of the day. Since female-headed families account for 92% of all welfare recipients, the lack of child care could be a major obstacle to the program. To solve this problem the federal Department of Health and Human Services suggests that some recipients' homes be designated as workfare sites for unlicensed child care, which welfare mothers would then be required to provide as their unpaid workfare "job"—regardless of their aptitude, training, or the conditions in their homes.

In any of its forms, workfare is nothing more than a politically acceptable form of harassment of welfare recipients. Case after case has shown that workfare saves money primarily by cutting off recipients who break program rules, rather than by placing them in jobs. In one New Jersey program, 2,879 recipients found jobs, while 9,016 lost benefits. In Ohio, 7% of workfare referrals went to work, but 32% were thrown off welfare. In a Michigan program no one got jobs; every single person who left welfare under the program was thrown off as punishment for failure to cooperate.[12]

Other programs for the poor are also under fire, though not always quite as intensely as welfare. In 1982 Congress passed only part of the cuts in Medicaid sought by Reagan; for 1983 the administration again proposes arbitrary limitations on total Medicaid funding. New proposals would require partial payment from patients for many formerly free services, reduce the share of some services picked up by the federal government, and cut former AFDC recipients off Medicaid one month, rather than four months, after they leave the welfare rolls.

The first round of Medicaid cuts were already bad enough for James Wilson. Retired after 50 years of work in the cotton and tobacco fields, he lives in a one-room shack outside Kingstree, South Carolina, supported by $260 a month from Social Security and $70 in food stamps. Wilson suffers from arthritis and heart problems, and needs six prescription drugs; Medicaid used to pay $110 of his $113 monthly drug costs. In early 1982 Wilson was told that because of the budget cuts, Medicaid would now only buy three of his six medicines. As a result he has been forced to make his own monthly choice: "Last month I buy my heart medicine. This month I buy my blood pressure medicine. Next month, I don't know."[13] Yes, Milton and Rose, we are indeed, free to choose.

New subsidized housing units authorized in 1982 fell to 150,000, about 25% below 1981 levels. Actual spending on housing will continue to rise through 1983 due to construction in progress on already authorized units (thus the increase in housing funds in Table 2). For 1983 and 1984, though, Reagan's budget-cutters are seeking no new authority for housing construction; in fact, they hope to cancel many housing projects previously authorized but not yet started. In other housing moves, rents in existing public housing would be increased, and rent subsidies for tenants in private housing would be capped, by the 1983 proposals.

Forgetting the Neediest

There are more services, and more tragedies, that could be described. But the picture is clear: the "truly needy," for whom Ronald Reagan periodically professes concern, are the biggest losers in the Great Budget Upheaval of 1981–?. They are 300,000 people who once had CETA jobs. They are millions of people who did not receive extended unemployment benefits. They are people who once qualified for food stamps, school lunches, welfare and Medicaid. They are people who could have moved into subsidized housing.

They are not the people who attend the glittering social events of Ronald Reagan's Washington, not the people who dine on Nancy Reagan's $209,000 china, not the people about whom *U.S. News & World Report* proclaimed, "Flaunting Wealth: It's Back in Style."[14] While Reaganomics is building a more perfect warfare state, it is also dismantling what there was of a welfare state.

For its most ardent supporters, this was the point all along. The right, new or old, has always been hostile to the notion of income redistribution, of providing benefits to the poor. Reagan's budget cuts are a key to solving inflation the conservative way, by driving down the wages, the working conditions and the bargaining strength of those at the bottom of the working class—those most dependent on government benefits for survival. Laid-off workers, deprived of unemployment checks, food stamps or welfare, will be forced to take any sweatshop job. Once at work, they will find any proposed pay cut or speed-up to be an offer they can't refuse. Wages will fall, profits will rise, price stability and economic growth can then be slowly restored. Someday the prosperity may even trickle down to those whose involuntary sacrifices made it possible.

Other budget cuts, less directly related to driving down wages, still reflect the same class prejudice. Federal funding of education is headed downward, with cuts in aid to disadvantaged students, to the handicapped, and to bilingual programs. In a move that will hit hard in many middle-income households, student loans and other funds for higher education have been slashed. "Thank God my parents got divorced," exclaimed Holly Koch, a junior at the University of Hartford in Connecticut. In the first year of Reaganomics she lost $500 of her work-study grant due to budget cuts, while her college costs rose $1500. If her parents had still been married, she would have lost even more. As it was, she was forced to work longer hours during the school year, while taking a full load of courses. If she was starting over, she said, "I'd go two years to community college" because it's cheaper.[15]

The cuts in transportation spending are almost entirely in mass transit and railroads, both of which are being phased out of the federal budget as rapidly as Congress will allow. The 1983 budget cuts highways more modestly, and airports even less. Throughout the country, use of public transportation has been increasing ever since gasoline prices took off in 1973; in Cleveland, for example, mass transit ridership rose 75% in five years.[16] The affluent gentlemen from the southern California suburbs who now command the heights of the federal government may not have thought clearly about what life in Manhattan, and other older central cities, would look like without mass transit—or they may not care.

Nothing could be more odious to a business-oriented administration, and specifically to a strip-mining fan like Interior Secretary James Watt, than squandering federal dollars on national parks, forests, pollution controls, new sewer systems, energy conservation, alternative energy development . . . down, down, down is the word for appropriations in all these areas. Budget cuts are helping to starve out regulatory agencies, speeding the task of deregulation (see Chapter 7).

There are limits, however, to the budget-cutting madness. Some things are sacred, even in the rapidly-declining energy budget. Of course we can't afford weatherization programs, solar energy research, or past levels of emergency fuel assistance to the poor—but the Clinch River breeder reactor remains on schedule. Like an aircraft carrier, it will cost more than $3 billion by the time it is ready to use in the 1990s; it would, however, be difficult to build an aircraft carrier in Tennessee, the home state of Senate Majority Leader Howard Baker. Kentucky's senators have managed to save federal funding for an even bigger synthetic fuels plant, with an eventual price tag of $4.5 billion. Because the technology is so experimental, the taxpayers are putting up 98% of the cost of this adventure—but will receive only 50% of the profits if the experiment succeeds.[17]

> I find it ludicrous to move fullspeed ahead with subsidies for Westinghouse and Boeing while at the same time gutting Head Start and other assistance to the poor. That's not just economically wrong, but politically foolish.
> —Congressman Jack Kemp[18]

Like David Stockman, Jack Kemp actually seems to have once believed that programs benefitting business would be cut along with everything else. Imagine their surprise on learning the real priorities of the Reagan administration. Washington provides a range of services to help the largest corporations export their products: loans, free advertising (called "export promotion"), regular reports on new market opportunities, etc. Stockman thought many of these programs could be abolished, as if they were no more valuable than, say, a lowly CETA job; he was quickly overruled by Commerce Secretary Malcolm Baldridge's appeal to the president.

Even some of the cuts in export loans that Reagan did approve were reversed in Congress. Nearly half of federal export loans finance overseas sales of U.S. aircraft, and more than 40% of the aircraft loans go to Boeing. The push to restore export loans was led by Senator Nancy Kassebaum, whose aide explained, "It made economic sense for our constituency in Kansas, where Boeing is such a large employer."[19]

Like the military, space exploration, and nuclear power, business services such as export promotion are too important to be cut back by a mere budget crisis. The weak claims of some clients appear to be alive and well and headed for ample funding.

The New Federalism: No Strings, No Funds

The form, as well as the content, of public spending is being changed. Amid great fanfare about states' rights and decentralization, Reagan is seeking to turn many federal programs over to state and local governments. Many formerly separate programs are being consolidated into a few block grants to be given to states and localities. The block grants come with no strings attached—and with distinctly lower funding, sometimes 25% lower, than the programs had before consolidation. An even grander scheme, Reagan's "New Federalism," calls for an elaborate decade-long process of transferring dozens of federal programs, and some accompanying sources of revenue, to the states.

Reactions from state and local officials have been overwhelmingly negative. The cut in funding that goes with the new block grants, it seems, has been widely noticed. "The situation is dismal," says Wilson Riles, California's superintendent of public education. "We have more freedom, yes, that's true. But it is almost exclusively the freedom to make the agonizing choices of where to cut."[20]

At first glance, the cut in funding may appear to be the only drawback of the block grant approach. Many of the old programs didn't work very well; part of Reagan's rhetoric about cutting through red tape and allowing greater local control will sound appealing to anyone who has tangled with federal agencies in the past. But beneath the rhetoric, the switch to block grants conceals some sweeping changes in the nature of federal programs.

Many of the now-consolidated programs were created by laws passed in the 1960s and early 1970s, in response to the demands of the civil rights, Black Power and welfare rights movements. The legislation creating the programs often reflected (to be sure, in a limited and distorted fashion) the politics of the times. Affirmative action requirements, funds targeted to particular low-income groups, community monitoring or feedback on programs—all these stipulations can be "untied" from federal money as the Reagan administration reorganizes social services.

Local control of block grants thus means that groups formerly protected by law are now pitted against each other in the struggle for shares of the smaller pie. In the harsher political climate of the 1980s, minorities and disadvantaged groups will find it much harder to win their battles over again. How much of the new education block grants will be spent on bilingual and special needs programs, and how much on computer courses that employers request to prepare the fastest students for their careers in Tomorrowland?

The same process would be taken much further by Reagan's New Federalism plan. Beginning in 1984, the federal government would take over the state share of Medicaid funding, while states would take over full responsibility for AFDC, food stamps, mass transit construction, and many other programs. Funding would at first come from a federal trust fund, into which Washington would deposit the revenues from federal alcohol, telephone and tobacco taxes, half the federal gasoline tax, and roughly half the crude oil windfall profits tax. After 1987 states would no longer be required to maintain current benefit levels, and federal taxes going into the trust fund would be phased out. Each state would be free to decide whether to levy its own taxes to support the programs, or to just skip it and enjoy the lower tax burden. You see, it isn't Ronald Reagan who is abolishing AFDC, food stamps and mass transit. If people fall for the New Federalism pitch, it will be fifty state legislatures that destroy these programs.

Early indications are, however, that very few people are falling for it. The response from state officials, Republicans and Democrats alike, has been generally chilly. One obvious flaw in the plan is that more than half the federal revenues going into the trust fund from 1984 to 1987 would come from the oil windfall profits tax. If this tax is then phased out, only the handful of oil-producing states would be in any position to replace it with state taxes. Most of the country would be left high and dry, forced to raise other taxes or to abolish programs all the faster.[21]

Even if it included only taxes that were equally accessible to all states, the New Federalism scheme would be biased toward elimination of the programs involved. States and cities already compete in offering tax breaks to lure corporate investment and jobs away from each other. The New Federalism would simply allow the stingiest states to up the ante in the great poker game of bidding for business. What state could dare to keep taxes high enough to finance food stamps, at the cost of losing a computer company to its neighbor? It is precisely in order to avoid this debasing spectacle that social service benefit levels, and the taxes that support them, should remain the responsibility of the federal government.

With luck, the New Federalism—and many of Reagan's proposed 1983 budget cuts—may never become law. Fun as it was demolishing useful government activities the first few times around, there are signs that the fascination is fading. Popular and Congressional resistance to further cuts in the same programs appears to be stiffening. Still, the iron laws of budgetary arithmetic have not been repealed. Either there will be huge federal deficits, or there will be tax increases, or there will be slower growth of the military, or the same programs will be hit again and again—or the major services to the elderly, above all Social Security, will finally be cut.

The latter is the choice of many conservative economists, if not yet of policymakers. There is a long-term media campaign underway to convince us that the financing of Social Security is fundamentally unsound, that big changes are needed soon to prevent catastrophe later. The argument has not yet persuaded most Americans, but it has already begun to sound familiar. It may be only a matter of time until more serious assaults are made on this largest, and hitherto most invulnerable, of social services. The most important question about future budget-cutting crusades, then, is: how serious are the financial problems of the Social Security system?

Coming of Age

Social Security may well be the most successful government program; recent budget battles certainly suggest that it is the most popular. It sends benefit checks to 35 million people, and accounts for 38% of the income received by the 65-and-older population. (Other government pensions provide another 8%, and public assistance 2%, making a total of 48% of all elderly income coming from the government.)[22]

No one lives a life of luxury on Social Security. In 1979 the monthly benefits averaged just under $300 for a retired single worker, under $500 for a retired couple. But thanks to the regular cost-of-living increases, benefits do keep up with inflation—more reliably than most savings, private pensions or even wages. Moreover, the massive Social Security system is managed with a minimum (by federal standards) of red tape and overhead expenses.

The bad news is that we are told the system is going bankrupt. For example, commenting on "Social Security's perennial financial crisis," *Business Week* declared that "By the end of 1982, the Social Security retirement fund will face a cash shortage, and by 1985 the annual shortfall in reserves will reach some $30 billion."[23] Such claims can be made because of the needlessly complex way in which Social Security is financed.

When you and your employer make payments to Social Security, the money is divided among three trust funds, for retirement, disability and hospitalization. Then when you retire, become disabled, or qualify for Medicare hospital benefits, your check is paid by the appropriate trust fund. The fact that they are called trust funds, and the natural sequence of first paying in, then getting money out later, seem to suggest that your payments have been saved and then paid back to you. Actually this has never been the case. The funds maintain only a small balance, often under a year's worth of benefits. Your payments now finance today's retirees; your retirement benefits later will be drawn from the taxes paid in by the people who are working at the time.

This "pay-as-you-go" approach had the advantage of allowing the system to start up almost immediately. The first Social Security legislation was passed in 1935, and the first benefit check was paid in 1940. The more cautious approach of saving each worker's contributions and then paying them back in benefits would have required waiting much longer, perhaps for decades, before beginning substantial payments. But "pay-as-you-go" financing runs into trouble in two situations: either when the country is suffering from inflation and unemployment, or when the elderly population grows faster than the number of employed workers.

The short-run troubles, both real and imagined, result from inflation and unemployment. Like the rest of us, Social Security does poorly in times of stagflation. Only employed workers (and their employers) pay into the trust funds, so when more people are out of work, less money comes into the Social Security system. Since benefit payments are increased to keep up with consumer prices, rapid inflation means rapid hikes in Social Security payments. Stagflation adds up to less money coming into the trust funds, and more money going out, a sure recipe for trouble. The economic problems of the last ten years or so, in other words, have driven the trust fund balances unusually low despite recent increases in the Social Security tax rate.

One implication of this is that the exact surplus or deficit in the trust funds at some time in the future cannot be projected with any certainty. You can make the numbers better or worse by varying your forecasts about inflation and unemployment. Thus, a few months after Reagan took office, the reported problems of Social Security suddenly got much worse. The new administrators assumed that double-digit inflation and 9% unemployment would last throughout Reagan's term in the White House—a far cry from the results of supply-side economics as optimistically forecast for public consumption.[24]

If President Reagan should manage to create a full-scale depression, he could indeed bankrupt Social Security along with much of the rest of the country. On more moderate assumptions, Social Security financing can be rescued for the early 1980s by allowing the three trust funds to borrow from each other. Only the retirement fund is actually broke, while the disability and hospital funds have sizeable surpluses. Interfund borrowing was the solution adopted by Congress, at least for 1982, after Reagan's first proposed cuts in Social Security were defeated. Once the short-run problems are survived, even the doomsayers agree that—quoting from *Business Week* again—events after 1985 "should put both the retirement and disability funds comfortably in the black until the second decade of the next century."[25]

In the inevitably fuzzy area of long-run forecasting, the decisive factor is the number of people expected to retire each year. Social Security finances should look good from perhaps 1985 to 2010 because the relatively small groups born between 1920 and 1945 will be retiring. After 2010 the much larger population born in the post-World War II baby boom will be retiring. At that point the ratio of people receiving benefits to people paying taxes into the trust funds will start to soar (unless there is another baby boom in the next decade, producing a surge of new workers by around 2010). By 2030 or so, almost all projections show Social Security, under its present system of financing, in serious trouble. Beyond that, presumably, either astronomical tax rates or lower benefits will be forced on us, if no major changes have been made in the system.

A Dependent By Any Other Name . . .

Are lower benefits inevitable? How much security can we afford for the senior citizens of the year 2030 (i.e., everyone reading this book in the 1980s who is still alive by then)? Whatever financing system is used, it is clear that retired people are ultimately fed and clothed by the labor of those who are currently working. But retired people are not the only ones in that position. Children are dependent on current workers in exactly the same way. So, too, are those working-age adults who, voluntarily or involuntarily, are out of work.

The costs of young and old dependents may even be similar: a West German study found the cost of raising a child to age 20 to be one-third to one-fourth greater than the cost of supporting the average 60-year-old for the rest of his or her lifetime.[26] Suppose, then, that we consider dependents of all ages as placing roughly equal burdens on the working population, and ask the broader questions: How many dependents per worker can we afford? How many will we have in the dreaded years beyond 2010?

Remarkably, it turns out that the standard Census Bureau projections of population trends imply that there will be *fewer* dependents per worker in the next century than there were from 1950 to 1970. The figures are shown in Table 3.[27] The table is based on the assumptions of a slight improvement in life expectancies, a "zero population growth" birth rate (close to the actual rate today), no net immigration, and continuation of the 1979 pattern that the number of workers is about three-fourths the number of people aged 18–64.[28]

Using these assumptions, we are headed toward a society with 1.34 dependents per worker—four dependents for every three workers, if you dislike fractional people. In 1960, when the baby boom generation was born but not yet working, there were 1.65 dependents per worker, or five for every three workers. (These figures for dependents include nonworking people aged 18–64: housewives, college students, disabled or unemployed workers, etc. However, the same pattern of fewer dependents per worker in the future than in 1960 can be found even if only young and old dependents are counted.[29])

Projecting the population decades into the future is an iffy business, of course. Nonetheless, the Census Bureau's best available guesses imply that the anticipated crisis in Social Security 30–50 years from now does not reflect any overall increase in the burden of dependents on the working population. If we could afford to live through the childhood of the baby boom generation, we can afford to live through its retirement.

The problem is that even if the overall burden is not increasing, the mix is changing. The dependent population used to include relatively more children and fewer senior citizens than it will in the future. There is no existing mechanism that smoothly transfers resources once spent on children—the pub-

**TABLE 3: WORKERS AND DEPENDENTS,
1950-2050 AND BEYOND**

Year	Percentage of Total Population That Is:				Dependents Per Worker
	0–17	65 +	18–64	Working	
1950	31.0	8.1	60.9	39.8	1.51
1960	35.7	9.2	55.1	37.8	1.65
1970	34.0	9.8	56.2	39.9	1.51
1979	28.4	11.2	60.4	44.9	1.23
2000	26.1	12.7	61.2	45.5	1.20
2025	24.0	18.2	57.8	43.0	1.33
2050	23.8	18.5	57.7	42.9	1.33
Long-Run Limit	23.4	19.0	57.6	42.8	1.34

Notes: The first three columns are based on actual Census data for 1950–1979, and on Census Bureau Series II-X projections for the future (see text for description of the underlying assumptions). Any society which maintains a zero population growth birth rate tends toward a stationary age distribution; that distribution, for the Series II-X assumptions, is shown here as the long-run limit.

The fourth column, for 1950-1979, is civilian employment plus Armed Forces employment as a percentage of total population of all ages. For the future, the 1979 ratio of people working to people 18-64 years old is assumed to continue.

The final column is simply calculated from the fourth column (i.e., dependents per worker is the reciprocal of the fraction of the population that is working, minus one.)

Source: Statistical Abstract of the United States, 1980, p. 30–31, and Economic Report of the President, January 1981, p. 264.

lic funds for education, and the private expenditures for diapers, bicycles and all the rest—into programs such as Social Security. According to the projections in Table 3, the ratio of children to working-age adults will be one-third lower in 2025 than it was in 1960. What will be needed, therefore, will be the transfer to senior citizens of roughly one-third the share of national income spent on children in 1960.

Such a shift of resources is not what the Reagan administration has in mind when it talks about solving the Social Security crisis. Like the current attacks on so many other services and benefits, the future attack on Social Security will have both a short-run budget-balancing goal and a long-run structural purpose.

The immediate budgetary problem is that the military buildup and the tax cut are leading to immense deficits. Rather than transferring funds from children to senior citizens, Reagan hopes to take money from both the young and the old, in order to pour it into the Pentagon and the widened tax loopholes for the rich. In the proposed 1983 budget, the major programs for the elderly absorb more than half of what's left after military spending and the interest on the national debt (see Table 2). Increasingly, there will be nowhere else for the budget-cutters to turn.

As the great national debate on slashing Social Security opens in 1983 or thereafter, considerable official effort will be put into concealing the fact that we are choosing between the elderly and the military. Social Security may well be the one program which, even today, can compete effectively with the Pentagon. Would voters still favor the MX missile, the B-1 bomber and our other costly methods of sending a message to Moscow, if they realized it all came at the expense of sending a retirement check to grandma?

Successful cuts in Social Security would do more for the Reagan administration than merely reducing the deficit. They would also assist the effort to find a profitable solution to inflation, to slow price rises by holding down wages, not profits. Lower Social Security benefits, like lower unemployment compensation or other government services, would make workers more insecure, more dependent on their employers, less willing to take the risk of speaking up and making demands about wages and conditions of work.

Lower retirement benefits, in particular, would make workers work longer. Until recently, the opposite has been happening: better benefits have been inspiring earlier retirement. The percentage of men aged 60 to 64 who were working or seeking work dropped from 83% in 1957 to 63% in 1977. At General Motors, where the United Auto Workers won a good private pension plan, the average age at retirement dropped from 70 in 1950 to 58 in the late 1970s.[30] Reversing these trends, making people work longer, would intensify competition for jobs: forcing everyone to work 50 years instead of 40 would increase the labor force by 25%. Moreover, it would be an increase in the labor force that did not involve any new training costs for employers.

In future installments of Reaganomics, then, the hope of an early or secure retirement may be scheduled to go the way of CETA jobs, extended unemployment benefits, food stamps and welfare: sacrificed in order to pay for the military and the tax cut, and to solve inflation by driving down the bargaining strength, and the living standards, of U.S. workers.

CHAPTER 6

Zapping Labor

We should look very closely at whether (unions) should not be bound, as business is, by the antitrust laws. Labor has become so powerful and, bargaining on an industry-wide basis as they do, I've thought for some time they should be subject to the same restraints that are imposed on industry and business.

—Ronald Reagan, April 23, 1980

Optimists might take heart from the fact that Reagan has not yet carried out his threat to use anti-trust laws to attack unions. They might note that he has denounced, but never actually moved to repeal, minimum wage laws, the Davis-Bacon Act (requiring payment of union wages on government construction projects), and other laws that protect labor.

But beyond lacking the courage of his worst convictions, the president has offered the trade unions very little ground for optimism. His choice of labor advisors appears to have been a calculated insult to union leaders. More substantively,

101

Reagan's policies have harmed organized labor in three major ways. First, the prolonged recession has weakened once-strong unions in heavy industry, forcing them to make unprecedented concessions to employers. Second, public employee unions have been intimidated both by budget cutbacks and by the example of Reagan's massacre of the air traffic controllers. Finally, organizing by many unions around occupational health and safety has been set back by the administration's deregulatory crusade.

This is no isolated insensitivity to the interests of organized labor. It is part of the grand design of Reaganomics, as important to the administration as slashing welfare and food stamps. The goal is to cure inflation and boost profits at the same time; the strategy for reaching that goal is to drive down wages and worsen working conditions, for those at the top as well as the bottom of the U.S. working class. At the bottom, harassing people off welfare and slashing food stamps, Medicaid, and housing subsidies will increase the number of desperate workers competing for the lowest-paying jobs. Although the minimum wage has not been literally abolished, the Reagan administration's quiet refusal to boost it along with inflation will make the $3.35 an hour minimum increasingly meaningless as time goes on.

At the top of the working class, meanwhile, recession ensures that many people will be driven out of their former "good jobs"; the administration calmly predicts that many laid-off auto and steel workers will never again be needed in their old industries. Cuts in trade adjustment assistance and other unemployment benefits pressure the jobless to give up, to seek lower-paying jobs rather than waiting for their previous employers to recover. For those who remain on the job, Reaganomics has created a climate in which one strong union after another must give back its past gains. It amounts to a violent worsening of the best wages and working conditions that labor has been able to achieve. Ten years ago a Nixon aide said that the purpose of wage-price controls was to "zap labor"; ten years later the politicians and the policies have changed, but the purpose remains the same.

For the unions the signals of bad news to come began almost immediately after the 1980 election, with Reagan's choice of his Secretary of Labor. In past administrations, from either party, it had been traditional to pick a labor secretary who was on speaking terms with at least some elements of union leadership—in the hopes of keeping open channels of communication. Reagan, however, picked an obscure, anti-labor businessman, evidently giving him the job as a reward for his efforts in the 1980 campaign.

Labor Secretary Raymond Donovan was formerly vice-president of Schiavone Construction, a medium-sized company in New Jersey. Schiavone turns out to have a checkered history: in the late 1970s it averaged ten citations a year from OSHA (the Labor Department's Occupational Safety and Health Administration) for "serious" safety violations involving "a substantial probability that death or serious physical harm could result." During Reagan's first year in office there were also two separate investigations into charges that Schiavone, with Donovan's knowledge, engaged in kickbacks to corrupt union officials and in payments to Mafia-related firms for jobs that were never performed.

At the time of his appointment Donovan was unknown to most national labor and business groups alike. More prominent nominees had been proposed by such Reagan supporters as the Teamsters (the only large union to back the Republican ticket in 1980), the U.S. Chamber of Commerce, the National Association of Manufacturers, and members of the Business Roundtable. Donovan was no stranger, though, to Republican Party politics. He was a top Reagan fundraiser and head of the Reagan campaign in New Jersey. Nor was he unknown in the world of far-right, anti-labor zealots: the National Right to Work Committee immediately hailed his appointment, and the *Washington Post* reported that Donovan might have given as much as $100,000 to the Washington Legal Foundation—a "public interest" law firm that specializes in attacking unions and government regulations.[1]

Other Labor Department officials are cut from the same cloth. OSHA director Thorne Auchter was vice-president of a Florida construction company which has been cited for 48 OSHA violations since 1972. Auchter was also director of special events for the Reagan campaign in Florida.[2] But the lack of ability to communicate with labor which these gentlemen display may not matter to the Reagan administration. There is no point in keeping channels of communication open unless you have something civil to say.

Driving Down the Auto Workers

The economic crisis that unfolded in the 1970s was catching up with even the strongest sections of labor by the beginning of the 1980s. After a decade of little or no real growth in many industries, energy price explosions, mounting competition from imports, and spiralling inflation, few unions were prospering. Reagan's economic policies proceeded to make a bad situation much worse, as the severe recession starting in 1981 led to massive layoffs and an epidemic of management demands for contract concessions.

Until recently the United Auto Workers was a perfect example of a powerful labor organization, just as the auto industry was a cornerstone of national prosperity. In 1978 new records were set for motor vehicle employment and production: one million workers made just over 13 million cars, trucks, and buses, and many of the parts for those vehicles. By mid-1980 both employment and production had dropped to about two-thirds of those record levels; there has been no recovery since. With the major companies losing billions of dollars, with jobs vanishing almost daily, the UAW has been driven into one setback after another: first, lower wages at Chrysler; next, local work rules changes in many plants; finally, cuts in wages and benefits at Ford and General Motors in early 1982.

The cause of this catastrophe was that suddenly no one wanted the giant cars that Detroit had so profitably produced for decades. Recession and high interest rates lowered auto sales, and the second oil crisis in 1979 sent those who could still afford cars scrambling after small, fuel-efficient models— many of them made in Japan. The imports were usually cheaper than similar domestic models, and in any case had developed a reputation for superior quality that kept them in demand. In December 1981 a sign in front of a joint Chevrolet-Saab dealership in the Boston area advertised "only" 89 Chevies and 1 Saab left over from the 1981 model year. National sales figures told a similar tale of disinterest in domestic makes.

U.S. auto companies should have seen that the crunch was coming. They had suffered through two costly warnings earlier in the decade: the first big wave of Toyotas and Datsuns, arriving around 1970, and then the panicked switch to smaller cars after the oil crisis of 1973–74. But from 1975 to early 1979 gasoline prices rose more slowly than the general rate of inflation; at some points prices at the gas pump actually fell. In retrospect it was an Indian summer of cheap gas. During those years consumers were once again willing to buy gas-guzzling big cars, and sales of vans and pickup trucks boomed. The industry invested billions of dollars outfitting its plants to produce the bigger vehicles it hoped to sell in the 1980s. Nine small car plants were switched back to making larger models. That investment of course proved to be pure waste when the next oil crisis struck in 1979.

So the auto slump is no simple result of high wages. It reflects the facts of recession, high interest rates, and a decade of disastrous corporate planning. Yet workers are being called on to solve the industry's problems by accepting wage cuts. At the end of 1981 Ford and GM were paying labor costs of close to $20 an hour—$12 in wages and $8 in benefits. That was said to be $8 an hour more than labor costs in auto plants in Japan, the source of over 80% of the imports.

The $20 an hour labor cost was a real cost paid by the companies, which did put them at a real competitive disadvantage. Much of it, though, consisted of costs which did not make the workers feel particularly affluent. One large chunk of the $8 in benefits is the cost of medical insurance and pension payments for retired UAW members. The total retirement cost is divided by the number of hours of work currently being done, to arrive at a cost per hour. When the industry is depressed, as it has been lately, the fixed total of retirement costs is spread over a smaller number of hours, boosting the hourly cost of benefits. If U.S. auto plants were running full blast like their competitors in Japan, thereby spreading the retirement costs over more hours of work, the $8 an hour of benefits might be reduced by as much as $2.

Another factor inflating benefits is the absurdly high cost of U.S. health care. General Motors is fond of saying that it spends more on health insurance than on steel. It less frequently points out that in Canada, a country with nationalized health care, the same medical benefits cost half as much—about $1 an hour less.[3]

Auto workers, in other words, do not feel like they are receiving $20 an hour. Wages of $12 an hour before taxes, while looking better than most workers' paychecks, do not make you exactly rich. Still, the pressure for auto workers to accept lower wages and benefits has proved irresistible. If the companies have their way, concessions will not be passed on in lower prices: according to *Business Week,* both GM and Ford officials "say that the companies intend to rebuild their profit margins before they start holding the line on price."[4] Those rebuilt profit margins will finance the industry's plans for retooling, using more and more robots, and fewer and fewer workers per car, in the attempt to keep up with the Japanese competition. The issue of job guarantees in exchange for wage and benefit concessions is likely to be one of the hottest topics in industrial union bargaining for the next several years.

Watching the Sun Set

For the building trades the slump started even earlier than for the UAW. In construction the end of the post-World War II economic boom brought on a long period of stagnation. As noted in Chapter 1, the value of new construction, corrected for inflation, grew rapidly before 1965, but slowed to an average of 0.5% annual growth from 1965 to its peak in 1978. The growth that did take place after 1965 was almost entirely in single-family housing, the area in which the building trades unions have always been weakest. All other private construction remained about constant, and government construction was cut back sharply. New highways and schools were no longer being built at the old rates, and nothing came along to replace them.

In short, changing patterns of government spending caused a decline in the large-scale construction projects on which the unions had flourished. This change followed an era in which unions had won sizeable wage increases; by the early 1970s hourly wages in construction were well ahead of even the leading sectors of manufacturing.

Relatively high wages in a suddenly declining industry led to efforts by employers to escape the unions' jurisdiction. Non-union companies sprang up, in many cases created as subsidiaries of unionized firms. The share of nonresidential construction done by union members dropped sharply.

The one bright spot for much of the 1970s, housing construction, took a plunge starting in 1979 when Jimmy Carter's efforts to control inflation sent mortgage rates soaring. While of less direct relevance to the unions, the housing slump has further depressed the job prospects for construction work in general.

Reaganomics offers more of the same. Funds for government building projects will be curtailed even more, with only slight increases in military construction. Despite campaign promises to the contrary, interest rates have stayed high enough, and consumer incomes low enough, to keep housing starts down. Barring the long-awaited supply-side miracle, construction, like autos, will remain depressed.

Lurking in the wings is the more frontal assault on the building trades favored by some Reaganites: repeal of the Davis-Bacon Act. That law requires payment of prevailing union wages on federally-funded construction projects; many states have similar laws modelled on it. Without Davis-Bacon the position of the building trades would be even bleaker. These unions may discover that their past history of conservatism is no defense against the tender mercies of a *real* right-winger in the White House.

The rest of industrial America is on the rocks for related reasons. In steel, autos and construction are normally the two biggest customers. There is immense worldwide excess capacity, and many other countries' steel mills are more modern and efficient, thanks to the U.S. failure to keep up with the latest foreign technologies in the 1950s and '60s.[5] U.S. Steel, the nation's largest producer (and among the most technologically sluggish in the past) has spent the last few years closing many of its steel mills and pleading poverty—only to borrow more than $6 billion to buy Marathon Oil in early 1982. As U.S. Steel executives discover the greater joys of being oilmen, more and more steel mills, and steelworkers' jobs, may be expected to disappear.

For trucking lines, auto and steel companies have traditionally been leading customers; other customers have been weakened by the recession as well. The Teamsters have been hurt not only by the slump in trucking, but also by the 1979 deregulation, which attracted a flurry of new, non-union firms to the industry—some of them newly-formed subsidiaries of old, unionized companies. (The past system of regulation, by making it hard for new firms to start up, allowed the established lines to pass on wage increases in higher rates with little fear of competition. Thus the Teamsters faced much less resistance at the bargaining table than they do today.)

Under these pressures the Teamsters' Master Freight Agreement, covering 300,000 truck drivers and warehouse workers, was renegotiated in early 1982. The union settled for three years of no wage increases except a scaled-back cost of living formula, and a change in work rules which may lead to further elimination of union jobs—in exchange for improved seniority safeguards for laid-off workers and a promise that unionized companies will stop establishing non-union subsidiaries.[6] Like the UAW settlement with the Big Three automakers, the Master Freight Agreement used to be of great importance in setting a pattern for other union contracts. For the early 1980s, at least, the message these former pace-setters are sending to other unions is hardly an encouraging one.

The picture is similar throughout other industries. In rubber, low auto sales, the switch to longer-lasting radials, and the pressure of competition from imported tires have flattened the industry. Workers at Goodyear and Uniroyal have agreed to concessions in wages, benefits and work rules in the hopes of saving their jobs. In meatpacking, United Food and Commercial Workers members at Armour, Wilson and Hormel renegotiated their contract nine months early, agreeing to a wage freeze in exchange for an 18-month moratorium on packinghouse closings.[7]

The White House has no plan for ending this decimation of once-healthy industries and unions. Indeed, according to the irrepressible David Stockman, this *is* the plan. As he told the U.S. Chamber of Commerce,

> High interest rates, unacceptable levels of current unemployment, the lost output we expe-

rienced last quarter and this quarter, the financial strains and the rising bankruptcies in the economy, and huge budget deficits that we are coping with—none of these are pleasant facts of life.

But they are all a piece of the same cloth. They are all part of the cure, not the problem. They are all a prelude to recovery, not evidence that the policies should be changed in some fundamental way.

Today's economic woes, said Stockman, are necessary evils that will help "end the curse of inflation once and for all."[8]

That is to say, the Reagan plan for heavy industry is to watch the sun set over the Midwest. The choice is one with long-run costs to the country: as plants are scrapped, as equipment is auctioned off, as experienced workers drift away, the old industries become less and less able to resume production in the future. But when workers move out of the old factory towns, their unions, and their union wages and work rules, do not move with them. From the standpoint of Stockman's Chamber of Commerce audience (the particular businessmen who are going broke, of course, excepted) that may look like a great way to end the curse of inflation.

Flying the Unfriendly Skies

A second area of labor movement strength has been the public employee unions. Government at all levels employs 16 million civilians, about one out of every six workers. (Contrary to the stereotype of swollen Washington bureaucracy, less than one-fifth of public workers are employed by the federal government. Three-fifths work for local governments, and more than one-fifth for states.) At least five million of these public employees are unionized: two million in the two principal teachers unions, one million in the American Federation of State, County and Municipal Employees (AFSCME), half a million in the postal workers unions, and many others. During the 1970s, while industrial unions experienced very little growth, the public employee unions boomed. From 1968 to

1978 AFSCME membership tripled, and the teachers unions doubled.[9]

These unions were bound to be weaker in the 1980s due to the spreading budget crises and cutbacks. One of the past sources of union strength was the fact of secure, growing employment throughout the government. But local tax revolts followed by Reaganomics have reversed this trend. In 1980, for the first time in over 30 years, public employment began to fall. From its all-time high in April 1980, the total government payroll had declined 600,000 by November 1981, and appeared to be headed further down. The layoffs, like the jobs, are primarily in local government, though cuts in federal and state funds formerly available to localities may often be responsible.[10]

Ronald Reagan has also sent public employees a more explicit message than mere cutbacks. If industrial unions have gotten a cold shoulder from the Reagan White House, government workers have received a knife in the back. The victim of the administration's assault was the Professional Air Traffic Controllers Organization (PATCO), one of the few unions to endorse Reagan in 1980. In October 1980, candidate Reagan wrote to PATCO President Robert Poli,

> You can rest assured that if I am elected President, I will take whatever steps are necessary to provide our air traffic controllers with the most modern equipment available and to adjust staff levels and work days so that they are commensurate with achieving a maximum degree of public safety. . . .
>
> I pledge to you that my administration will work very closely with you to bring about a spirit of cooperation between the President and the air traffic controllers.

Less than a year later—on August 3, 1981—President Reagan fired PATCO's membership en masse for daring to strike.

Though the ending was all Reagan's, the beginnings of the PATCO strike stretch back almost a decade earlier. The Federal Aviation Administration, the agency that employs the air controllers, realized in the early 1970s that it had a morale problem in the control towers, and paid a Boston University consulting team $2.8 million to study it. The consultants' report, delivered in 1978, blamed outdated, harsh management methods for poor morale. (For instance, on a standardized test used to determine employees' attitudes toward their bosses, the controllers rated their supervisors' "tolerance of freedom" lower than any other group tested—even lower than soldiers rate their Army officers.) The consultants recommended that a "program be undertaken with joint union-management co-operation to improve work life." The FAA, instead, began planning to combat a strike.

The job of air traffic control is a very tense one. It involves long hours of staring at a radar screen and issuing orders to make sure that none of the blips come too close to each other. It has been compared to playing a "Space Invaders" video game, with the difference that if you let two dots on the screen collide, you lose a lot more than your quarter.

The working conditions had been getting worse in the years leading up to the strike. Air traffic increased 20% from 1978 to 1981, while the number of controllers and the level of control tower equipment remained the same. Whenever traffic piled up at an airport, the controllers were under pressure from their supervisors to get the planes moving faster—which could only be done by violating federal safety rules and allowing planes to land or take off too close together.

The job takes its toll on the workers' health and personal lives: controllers have above-average rates of ulcers, alcoholism, divorce and other problems traceable to stress. The hours, too, are destructive of family life. At some airports controllers work two days, two evenings, and one "graveyard shift" every week. Only 11% of them last to retirement age, despite an easy retirement policy (controllers can retire after 25 years of service at any age, or after 20 years if over 50). In recent years, half the people leaving the job have done so for medical reasons.

PATCO endorsed Reagan in 1980, in fact, because of hostility to Carter's FAA chief, Langhorn Bond, the man the controllers viewed as responsible for the speed-up of their work. Little did they know that Reagan would continue the hated Carter-Bond policies, with two new twists. One was Reagan's decision to answer the strike with immediate firings; Carter had planned warnings that firings were imminent. The other, less visible but equally important, was the new flight reduction plan. In the crucial weeks just before the strike, Reagan's men at the FAA worked out a plan for reduction in flights that made the major airlines happy. PATCO was unaware of this, and expected that pressure from the airlines would help force a rapid settlement.

By the time of the PATCO strike the airline industry was in need of help from someone. It made almost no money in 1980, and lost about $200 million in the first half of 1981. The problems were in part due to the 1979–80 rise in fuel prices, and in part to the 1978 Airline Deregulation Act. Freed of FAA controls over routes and rates, and inexperienced at "free market" competition, the airlines overextended themselves, adding many new routes without cutting out less profitable old ones. By 1981 most planes were flying with more than half their seats empty.

The established airlines were also shaken by competition from the no-frills, cut-rate carriers, like New York Air and People Express on the East Coast and Midway Air in the Midwest, that sprang up after deregulation. Underselling the major airlines, New York Air captured 25% of all Boston-New York-Washington air traffic in its first six months. At least five more such lines had planned to start up in late 1981.

The FAA's flight reduction plan may well deliver a death blow to the no-frills lines, and save the major airlines from their own overextension. Airport traffic was reduced by 25% overall, but by 50% at the busiest airports at rush hours. Within those guidelines all existing airlines were free to apportion the cutbacks as they saw fit. This means that no new lines can start up; it forces each airline to prune the least profitable 25% of its flights; and it falls most heavily on rush-hour flights at the biggest airports, the specialty of the no-frills lines. Within a few months of the PATCO strike and FAA flight reduction plan, for example, New York Air had to give up flying from New York to Boston, formerly one of its top markets.

The two years the FAA says it needs to rebuild the air traffic control system without PATCO thus can be translated as a two-year breather from competition for the established airlines. They get a chance to drop their least profitable routes, to scrap their oldest planes, to lay off employees—all the while blaming it on PATCO. Other powerful interest groups are much less happy: military, corporate and private flights were cut back much more sharply than scheduled airlines, leading to a bit of clamoring from the business community for rehiring some PATCO members and lifting the flight restrictions. But the alliance of the White House and the major airlines has been enough to uphold the FAA's flight reduction plans so far.[11]

At considerable cost to the smooth functioning of the nation's airports (and to 11,000 fired controllers), Ronald Reagan has made his feelings about public employee militance perfectly clear: if you strike, don't expect to come back. The message has not been lost on other public employees and employers. Postal workers, voting on a contract soon after the PATCO strike began, accepted it overwhelmingly; many had planned to vote against the contract but said Reagan's firing of the controllers changed their minds. Across the country, state and local government officials rushed to announce that striking public employees would be fired and replaced.

In the 1920s, in the days of Reagan's idol Calvin Coolidge, employers fired people for union activities, hired strike-breakers, and made workers sign "yellow-dog" contracts promising not to join a union. Today the Reagan administration has signalled its willingness to see such tactics return. New air traffic controllers hired since the strike have been forced to sign a pledge that they will not engage in any job actions such as sick-outs or slowdowns, let alone strikes.

Deregulating Workers' Health[12]

As well as tilting the bargaining table against industrial and public employee unions, the Reagan administration has been attempting to pull the floor out from under a promising new development in many parts of the labor movement. Health and safety organizing was one of the trade unions' success stories of the last decade. It was made possible by the 1970 passage of a union-backed law which created the Occupational Safety and Health Administration (OSHA). Since its beginning

OSHA has been continually attacked by industry—but before Reagan the attackers were always firing at OSHA from the outside. Now, with committed opponents of regulation running the agency, the administration has gutted and delayed critical OSHA standards, whittled away at guidelines for inspection and enforcement, and censored educational materials produced under OSHA grants.

Under the OSHA law employers have a "general duty" to provide a workplace "free from recognized hazards that are causing or likely to cause death or serious physical harm to employees." They also must meet OSHA's more specific standards. To guarantee compliance OSHA has the power to inspect workplaces, make citations for violations and propose penalties.

The law promises more than OSHA has ever delivered. Even in the heyday of the agency, the sting was taken out by a low enforcement budget, an appeals process which routinely favors management, low penalty fines, and the partially successful effort to return enforcement and inspection to state governments. OSHA inspected less than 2% of all worksites per year; the total of all OSHA fines averaged around $4 million a year in the early 1970s, strictly a petty cash item on the balance sheets of corporate America. The Chamber of Commerce estimated that for most of the 1970s the cost of modifying plants and equipment to meet OSHA standards averaged around $3.5 billion a year, or 2.5% of corporate profits.

What really has industry up in arms is not the immediate economic cost of OSHA, but rather the political impact it has had on the labor movement. The establishment of the legal right to a healthy and safe work environment, even if poorly enforced, is a gain for workers. Unions like the Oil, Chemical and Atomic Workers, the UAW and others have used the law to attack hazards in their industries.

In bringing health and safety to the union agenda, OSHA has stimulated organizing drives across the country. In the South, the debilitating effects of cotton dust and its link to brown lung disease sparked massive efforts to organize the textile industry. In northern California, a drive to unionize electronics workers has focused on the dangers of the chemicals used to manufacture computer chips. The occupational hazards associated with office work have been central to the movement to organize clerical workers.

Reagan's OSHA director, Thorne Auchter, was quick to begin reversing the advances labor had made in health and safety. First he gutted a number of OSHA regulations scheduled to go into effect in 1981. Then he withdrew from consideration some proposed regulations the Carter administration had never acted on, while placing other rules "under policy review" or "subject to reconsideration."

A walk-around pay regulation, for example, would have required employers to pay workers their regular wages for assisting OSHA inspectors surveying the plant. Scheduled to take effect in mid-1981, it was revoked by Auchter.

Another proposed regulation would have required all toxic chemicals in a workplace to be labelled with their generic names. This proposal was immediately withdrawn by Auchter. Instead, serious consideration is being given to an alternative suggested by Exxon: chemicals could be marked with a five-color code indicating degrees of harmfulness. This would certainly liven up factory decor. The problem is that if a bottle said, for instance, "trichloroethane," workers could seek outside opinions on its dangers; if instead it says "green-hazard level 3" there is no way to question the company's judgment of the risks involved.

During the Carter years workers were given access to all company medical and exposure records relating to harmful substances used in the plant. But industry now claims this openness could result in trade secrets being leaked to competitors, and Auchter is considering a rule allowing companies to sue workers if such leaks ever do occur.

Auchter and his staff are pushing to apply "cost-benefit analysis," a supposedly objective standard, to all regulations. The idea is that the cost to employers of complying with a regulation can be weighed against the benefits of the regulation. If the costs are greater, the regulation gets canned.

But industry spokesmen, and their friends who now control the federal government, are notoriously inclined to overstate some of the costs and overlook some of the benefits of regulation. The most important benefits of regulation are reductions in injuries, illnesses or deaths. To weigh these against business costs, a dollar value must be placed on human life and health—a difficult task, to say the least. (More on this problem in the next chapter.) Occupational health advocates fear that industry, by padding its costs and slighting the health benefits, will use cost-benefit analysis to "prove" almost all standards should be abolished.

The 1981 Supreme Court decision upholding OSHA's cotton dust standard was a major legal test of the cost-benefit approach. The Court rejected industry's argument that the costs of lowering cotton dust levels in factories outweighed the benefits, and ruled that OSHA need only consider the technological "feasibility" of meeting its health standards, not the cost.

Robert Coleman, of the cotton and textile industry trade association, was nonplussed. He claimed that the Supreme Court did not outlaw the use of cost-benefit methods: "All that the Court did say was that the law does *not require* OSHA to use that analysis." Thorne Auchter agreed, saying that "cost-effectiveness" studies could still be used to determine "what particular methods (will) achieve the required levels of protection" against cotton dust.

At present the textile industry has until 1984 to make the engineering changes necessary to bring dust levels down to the OSHA standard. In the meantime, the Amalgamated Clothing and Textile Workers Union thinks Auchter may try to revoke the standard so that industry does not have to make the changes. OSHA might come to agree with the industry contention that forcing textile workers to wear masks and respirators is more "cost-effective" than improving plant ventilation.

Many textile workers claim that masks are uncomfortable, and ineffective in keeping dust out of the lungs besides. In an interview Auchter responded that, "well, employers are asked to do things....under OSHA that aren't always comfortable for them."

To ease the discomfort felt by employers, Auchter is using what he calls the "performance approach" to measuring occupational hazards. He says this means "we set forth a strict regulatory goal, but at the same time permit employers flexibility in how they achieve it."

OSHA's noise standard, for instance, sets a strict regulatory goal: no worker is to be exposed to an eight-hour average of more than 85 decibels. But the performance approach means that employers may choose any method they see fit in measuring noise levels. They can monitor the noise exposure of individual workers, or exposure at a particular work station, or general levels of noise in the entire plant. Indeed, it might be cost-effective to try out all these approaches and select the one that gives the lowest result.

Even more drastic changes in procedures were under discussion in OSHA in late 1981, including:

*Exempting from OSHA inspections any company whose records show a number of lost workdays due to on-the-job injuries below the national average for manufacturing;

*Exempting companies which set up labor-management safety committees;

*Waiving penalty fines for first-time violations, and for companies which correct violations within the time stated in the citations;

*Informing employers of worker complaints and allowing "voluntary compliance" in fixing reported hazards before scheduling inspections.

The AFL-CIO says these changes, if carried out, would "disembowel OSHA."

OSHA's efforts at worker education have been slashed as well. Films, pamphlets and slide shows prepared under the Carter administration have been recalled and destroyed. The New Directions program, which gave grants to unions, labor education centers, universities, and the Council on Occupational Safety and Health (COSH) groups in many cities, is being cut back sharply if not eliminated. In general, the gains which OSHA represented for labor are being systematically destroyed in the new crusade for deregulation.

*****

The targets of Reaganomics are widely scattered. They include people whose paths never cross, people inclined to be suspicious of each other. The lives once rooted in $12 an hour assembly line jobs, the security of working for the government, union campaigns to rid factories of cancer-causing chemicals, are a world apart from those shaped by welfare, food stamps, public housing projects. Yet neither is the cause of the other's problems; neither is prospering under the current regime. Both are under attack, and for the same reason: Ronald Reagan's solution to the economic crisis requires driving down labor costs—worsening wages and working conditions for both the top and the bottom of the U.S. working class.

CHAPTER 7

The Smell of Success

Avoiding defects is not costless. Those who have low aversion to risk—relative to money—will be most likely to purchase cheap, unreliable products. Agency action to impose quality standards interferes with the efficient expression of consumer preferences.

—from a 1980 report co-authored by James C. Miller III, who is now chairman of the Federal Trade Commission.

Unfettered free enterprise is all the rage in Washington these days. But hearing that the head of the FTC had advocated the freedom to sell junk to poor people was an embarrassment even to the administration's friends in business. "It's crazy," said a U.S. Chamber of Commerce executive. "Industry is not in favor of making defective products—think of the product liability suits—and it has no intention of doing so."[1]

Industry definitely is in favor, however, of the bulk of Reagan's program of deregulation. The theory is that de-

119

regulation, together with tax cuts and budget cuts, will free business to expand its profits, production and employment. While regulatory bodies throughout the federal government are under fire, the attack is concentrated most heavily on a handful of newer agencies—such as OSHA, the Environmental Protection Agency (EPA), the Consumer Product Safety Commission (CPSC), and the National Highway Traffic Safety Administration (NHTSA)—and on the Interior Department's restrictions on private use of federal lands.

The most remarkable fact about these regulations is that by so many standards they have been successful. At least four kinds of evidence confirm this success. First, even the rather mechanical cost-benefit analysis favored by administration economists seems to show the newer regulations are worthwhile. Second, the much-touted paperwork burden created by regulations turns out to be quite small. Third, many businesses have developed new lines of profitable production in response to regulations. Finally, there is direct evidence of declining levels of pollution in the years since environmental regulation began.

This is not to say that all government rules are sensible or worth preserving. But the occasional attack on obviously silly rules is only the loss-leader of the deregulatory sales pitch, a throwaway designed to attract popular support. In a press conference on November 10, 1981, for example, Reagan described the case of Katie Beckett, a partially paralyzed three-year-old who had been in a hospital since the age of four months. Although Katie could receive better and cheaper care at home, Social Security's Supplemental Security Income program would only pay her medical bills if she remained hospitalized.

On November 12, Health and Human Services Secretary Richard Schweiker waived SSI rules to allow Katie to return home without loss of benefits, making Katie and her parents much happier as well as saving the government money. Two months later, when asked whether there had been other waivers of the rules in cases similar to Katie's, a Social Security official said, "That decision applied to her only, and there have been no other exceptions made."[2]

Katie's story scored a rhetorical point for the Reagan administration. But it is not for the sake of other people like her that regulations are being rolled back.

Count It Again, Murray

While denunciation of silly rules may create the impression that there are no real benefits of regulation, a new brand of statistics-mongering suggests that there are immense costs. "More than $100 billion a year!" is the most common version of the burden said to be imposed on business. A closer look at the argument behind this figure, however, reveals that very little of the supposed $100 billion cost results from newer social regulatory agencies—and that the measurable financial benefits of the newer agencies' rules well outweigh their costs.

The top professional economist in the Reagan administration, Council of Economic Advisors chairman Murray Weidenbaum, specializes in writing about the costs of regulation. In a 1979 article he said, "It is hard to overestimate the current rapid expansion of government involvement in business in the United States." Yet he seems to have risen to that difficult task. His studies are the source of the $100 billion cost estimate for regulations. Furthermore, he claims that four-fifths of federal regulatory budgets are devoted to "the newer areas of social regulation, such as job safety, energy and the environment, and consumer safety and health."[3]

Another economist, William Tabb, has examined Weidenbaum's studies and found them to be, in polite terms, shoddy. For example, Weidenbaum counted as "newer areas of social regulation" not only the Food and Drug Administration (created in 1931), but also the Coast Guard, the Customs Service, the Bureau of Alcohol, Tobacco and Firearms, and many other agencies which are neither new nor socially oriented.

Weidenbaum employed a unique and arbitrary "multiplier" method to arrive at his $100 billion figure. He assembled separate estimates of the amounts spent to comply with various agencies' regulations in 1976. The total of these costs was 20 times the budgets of the agencies. So for all later years he simply multiplied the agency budgets by 20 to arrive at the cost of compliance. By including the Coast Guard and the like, he got the total agency budgets up to $5 billion by 1979, hence the $100 billion "cost" to business.

Even accepting the multiplier method, Tabb showed that this figure is a wild overstatement. Reorganizing Weidenbaum's data to focus on the 11 social regulatory agencies created since 1960, Tabb found that the costs they imposed on business in 1976 were 6.6 times the agencies' budgets, not 20 times. The 1979 budget total for the 11 agencies was slightly under $1.8 billion, so Weidenbaum's own methodology implies that the cost to business of the "newer areas of social regulation" was under $12 billion.

Looking at the costs of regulation alone, without considering the benefits—as Weidenbaum and other advocates of deregulation often do—has been compared to "measuring the pain of a hypodermic needle without considering the value of the injected penicillin." Many of the benefits of regulation are hard to measure in dollars: what value should be placed on avoiding illnesses, injuries and deaths? Economists have tried, nonetheless, to estimate the monetary worth of such benefits, often by counting insurance premiums, medical expenses and lost wages as the cost of illness or injury. It should be noted that this approach is far from satisfactory. The "cost" of an injury in lost wages is greatest if it happens to a white male, for instance. Moreover, the economists' estimates completely fail to capture the non-financial, human impact of disability or death.

Still, for whatever they are worth, there are many studies estimating the benefits created by government regulation. A survey of this literature produced a best guess of $21 billion in annual benefits from the Clean Air Act in 1978. A similar figure for water pollution regulations is $12 billion (most of the benefits in this case being improved recreational use of rivers and lakes). Reduced numbers of deaths due to auto safety standards may be "worth" $6 billion a year, and reduced workplace accidents worth $10 billion. So these four areas alone, which are not the only benefits resulting from the newer regulatory agencies, were estimated by economists to be worth $49 billion a year—or more than four times the costs imposed by the whole group of 11 newer agencies in Tabb's calculation.[4]

The burden of paperwork has of course become legendary among businessmen grumbling about the need for regulatory relief. More than a third of Weidenbaum's estimated costs of regulations consist of paperwork done to comply with federal rules. However, the government's 1976 study of paperwork requirements, which Weidenbaum relies on, found that two-thirds of the time spent by all businesses filling out forms for federal regulators was due to a single agency, the Federal Communications Commission. The daily logs of programs, operations and maintenance which the FCC demanded from radio and television stations simply dwarfed the efforts of any other agency.

(Does that sound implausible? It did to me, so I called a radio station manager to check. She confirmed that the FCC did require incredibly detailed daily logs, and was amazed that other industries did not have to keep similar records. She felt that some of the logs would be kept by the station for its own records even without regulations, some were used by the FCC to check on fairness, "equal time" and community service broadcast standards, and some probably fell into the category of silly rules.)

Whether it served a useful purpose or not, the huge FCC paperwork load is on its way to being a thing of the past, as the Reagan administration moves to deregulate broadcasting. In contrast with the FCC's former appetite for paper, four leading newer social agencies (EPA, OSHA, CPSC and NHTSA) together were responsible for just over one percent of all paperwork required by federal regulators in 1976.[5]

More evidence that the paperwork burden is mainly mythical comes from a dissenting voice within the business community. Jewell Westerman is vice-president of a management consulting firm that studies the efficiency of corporate bureaucracies. He reports that, of the more than 200 companies his firm has studied, not one would achieve significant labor savings if regulatory paperwork requirements were lifted. He points out that Goodyear's trumpeted complaint about spending 34 employee-years annually filling out reports for the government should be compared to Goodyear's total payroll of 154,000. Getting rid of 34 jobs would be a trivial 0.02% reduction in labor costs for the company.

Westerman argues that padded corporate bureaucracies making unnecessary work for their subordinates are much more important obstacles to improvement in productivity and profits. He mentions a large bank which was spending 300 times as much labor answering internal inquiries from executives as it was on making commercial loans. Another large company spent $900,000 a year for six years producing an elaborate computer report which went to only one senior executive—who never read it, only initialed it and gave it to his secretary to file. Beside such private-sector sources of waste, concludes Westerman, the worst efforts of Washington look pale by comparison.[6]

Pollution vs. Profits

Squawking from big business and its friends to the contrary, the environmental regulations of the 1970s often led the way to increased profits for the regulated companies. Examples can be found in many affected industries, though perhaps most frequently in chemicals. For instance, the ban on flourocarbon aerosol sprays prompted American Cyanamid's Miss Breck division to develop a new spray can, free of fluorocarbons, that was cheaper than aerosols. Conoco's coal trains used to scatter coal dust over the countryside, losing tons of coal per trainload; pollution controls forced them to stop that loss. Ordered to control air pollution from its factories, General Motors developed new boilers that made the air cleaner and also cut the factories' fuel bills. DuPont used to dump iron chloride wastes into the ocean until the EPA found out about it; now the company reprocesses and sells iron chloride at a profit, just as its competitors had been doing all along.

In at least two cases dire predictions have been made that entire industries would be ruined by regulations—and the industries have gone on to prosper. Polyvinyl chloride (PVC) is one of the most widely used plastics, found in phonograph records, bottles, food wrappings, and hundreds of other common products. It is made from vinyl chloride (VC), a gas which was discovered to be a potent cause of cancer in the early 1970s. OSHA responded in 1975 by lowering the allowable exposure of workers to 1 part per million of VC in the air, down from the 500 parts per million formerly permitted.

Consulting firms studying the VC standard for OSHA and for the plastics industry predicted that it would cost $90 billion and lead to the loss of more than two million jobs. Actually, nothing of the sort happened. B.F. Goodrich, a leading producer, developed new production techniques that plugged many leaks and reduced VC waste sharply, for a cost to the company of only $34 million. Moreover, Goodrich found the new techniques cut labor costs, and could be leased to other companies. From 1975 to 1978 the VC/PVC industry grew more than twice as fast as U.S. manufacturing in general, and four major new producers entered the market.

Similarly, the EPA feared that its tough standards limiting the dumping of toxic wastes into municipal waterworks could put as many as 20% of all electroplating firms out of business. But again, the regulation forced the development of new methods of recycling wastes. One Milwaukee electroplating company found that the equipment needed to comply with the toxic waste standard would pay for itself in recycled water and chemicals within 2½ years.[7]

Environmental regulations, of course, are not just good for particular businesses. They are also responsible for noticeable reductions in some (not all) forms of air and water pollution. During the 1970s particulate emissions (soot, dust, etc.) into the air fell by one-half, and sulfur dioxide by one-sixth. The newest cars were much cleaner than their predecessors; even the average pollution per mile, for all old and new cars on the road, dropped by one-third to one-half over the decade.[8] Bodies of water such as Lake Erie, the Willamette River in Oregon, the Detroit River, the Connecticut River and many others, saw increasing signs of life, reversing the trend of earlier years. The Cuyahoga River in Cleveland was no longer capable of catching fire, as it once did. While pollution was by no means stopped in the 1970s, it was definitely pushed back—by some of the regulations that are now under the sharpest attack.

There's No Success Like Failure

So far we have seen that the newer areas of regulation are producing monetary benefits worth many times their cost, imposing no significant paperwork burden on business, stimulating profitable new innovations, and achieving measurable success in reducing pollution. Why, then, are so many people saying such terrible things about these rules?

This question can be answered on several levels. Most immediately, many regulations do not lead the affected companies into more profitable methods of production. A corporation forced to control air pollution from its factories will gain little comfort from the knowledge that the health benefits to society outweigh the costs of anti-pollution devices. The costs show up on the company's balance sheet; the benefits do not. What is true for society as a whole therefore—that the health benefits are greater than the costs of controls—is not true for the corporations that must install the controls.

Beyond the immediate threat of any particular regulation, there is the general problem for business that if regulations are accepted as legitimate and useful, they will continue to spread. New standards for pollution control, for product safety, for occupational health, will keep on cropping up. Even if your company has not yet been harmed by such rules, you may want to join the crusade against regulation as a form of insurance policy for the future.

Going still further in this direction, rhetoric about the failure of regulation sometimes conceals a deep-seated fear of the very fact of regulatory success. The belief that all social problems are solved best by the market, that businesses must be left free to do as they choose as often as possible, is an article of faith for the right wing. What greater heresy could be imagined that the idea that corporations create problems and the federal government is reasonably effective in solving them? If this notion becomes widespread, it may not stop with things like pollution: voters may demand controls on prices, standards for socially useful investments . . . clearly, a dangerous line of thought. Better to head it off before it starts, by claiming that even the controls on pollution were unsuccessful and ill-advised.

Many of these themes can be seen in one of the most important cases of regulation: auto safety and pollution standards. Nine months into the Reagan administration, the *New York Times* asked General Motors chairman Roger B. Smith what deregulation meant for GM. The reporter summarized the answer as "not much yet," but noted that Smith

takes satisfaction in the realization that, if GM
hasn't felt much of the impact of deregulation,
at least it need no longer fear adoption of new
regulations. "If nothing else," he said, "our
hearts are lighter."

Smith claimed that pollution control equipment added
$725 to the cost of a car, and safety devices another $400—a
noticeable chunk of the $8,900 average price of a new car in
1981. If all environmental and safety regulations had been
eliminated at once, and if GM had then chosen to remove all
those features from its cars and pass on the entire savings to
consumers, the price would have fallen by $1,125 per car. GM
would have sold more cars, boosted its profits, and perhaps
rehired a few laid-off employees (though it would also have had to
find new jobs for the workers who used to put in anti-pollution
and safety devices.) But the hidden costs to the public of those
deregulated cars—the illnesses, injuries and deaths caused by
increased air pollution and more fatal traffic accidents—would
add up to much more than $1,125 per car.

Even the Reagan administration could not undo all regulations overnight. But it did start out with a verbal bang,
announcing in April 1981 that it planned to ease 34 auto-related
regulations. The three most important, according to Roger
Smith, were the elimination of the requirement of air bags or
other passive safety restraints in future model years, the rollback of emission standards to 1980 levels, and the reduction
of the speed at which bumpers must be able to survive a crash
undamaged from 5 to 2½ miles per hour. Of these three,
however, only the elimination of the air bag rule was actually
carried out during 1981, leading Smith to begin mentioning his
impatience to the press.

The costs of *de*regulation are revealed in two of Smith's
favorite changes. GM says it will save $500,000 a day thanks
to the abolition of the air bag regulation. Accepting that figure,
the total savings to all U.S. automakers over four years will
be roughly $1.5 billion. In contrast, William Nordhaus (a mem-
ber of the Council of Economic Advisors in the Carter administration) calculates that consumers will end up paying $4.5
billion in medical costs, insurance costs and lost wages due to

deaths and injuries caused by the lack of air bags in the next four model years' cars. Roger Smith, needless to say, will pay very little of that $4.5 billion.

GM also claims that consumers would save $100 per car from the lighter bumpers that could be used under the 2½ m.p.h. crashworthiness standard—resulting from the lower purchase price and the fuel savings due to the car's lighter weight. But almost any trip to an auto body shop costs more than $100. So if the heavier bumper saves you from just one accident that requires body work during the lifetime of the car, it is more than worth the price.[9]

Few other consumer products are as heavily regulated as autos. Much of the business bellyaching about regulations focuses instead on types of investment that are required or prohibited by federal rules. Investments required for pollution control amounted to $7 billion in 1979, or 4% of all business spending on new plants and equipment. It is a significant cost, if not quite the life-or-death matter it is sometimes made out to be.

But the anti-pollution costs were concentrated in a few areas: public utilities and the petroleum industry together spent $4 billion of the $7 billion total, amounting to over 8% of new investment in both these branches of the energy business. A few other industries, such as steel and paper, also had to allocate large fractions of their investments in the late 1970s to stopping pollution. To a remarkable extent, though, the burden of pollution control investment is a burden on the energy industry.[10]

The Good, The Bad, The Oily

For the energy industry, the stakes are far higher than a paltry (to them) $4 billion annual investment. They are seeking the "freedom," formerly denied them, to drill oil and gas, strip-mine coal, and build pipelines, power plants and refineries wherever they want, whatever the environmental impact—a freedom which means many billions for them, and disaster for the air-breathing, water-drinking public.

Long accustomed to advance planning, the oil industry got its regulatory wish list for the Reagan years written up earlier than other interest groups. Back in August 1980 the American Petroleum Institute—Big Oil's lobbying and public relations outfit—published *Two Energy Futures,* their plan for the '80s. The two futures are the bad one, in which the country continues its past course of importing more and more OPEC oil, and the good one, in which the energy industry is given free rein to produce more oil, gas and coal in the U.S., cutting oil imports in half over the decade.[21]

The API has two major recommendations about how to achieve the good future instead of the bad one. First, open up federal lands and the federally controlled Outer Continental Shelf for more oil and gas drilling and coal mining. Second, make environmental regulations more "flexible"; the Clean Air Act, in particular, is targetted for intensive flexing. These two points have moved to the top of Big Oil's Washington agenda, replacing, at least for a while, concerns about windfall profits taxes, nuclear power, synfuels, or the speed of price decontrol.

The two oil industry proposals are entirely in line with the Reagan administration's biases. Interior Secretary James Watt is an enthusiastic advocate of opening federal lands to private developers. Watt's previous job, in fact, was as president and chief attorney of the Mountain States Legal Foundation, a group funded by large energy and mining companies, which brings lawsuits to support land developers and block environmental regulations.

The American Petroleum Institute's preferred energy future, therefore, is well on its way to becoming reality. It's worth taking a look at how they think it will work—and what their idea of success would smell like.

The API notes that U.S. oil and gas production declined throughout most of the 1970s. But it believes that more rapid exploration would allow present levels of production to continue through 1990. The oilmen are especially bullish on coal output, which they project as at least doubling during the '80s. (Oil companies own many of the largest coal companies.) They hope, somewhat nervously, that all nuclear plants presently on order or under construction will be completed within the decade. Add that to some modest beginnings of commercial synfuels and renewable energy sources, continuing progress in conservation—and, sure enough, only about half the 1980 levels of oil imports would be needed by 1990.

In the search for oil and gas, much of the U.S. has been exhaustively explored. One-fifth of the country's total land area is either producing oil and gas or under lease for exploration. At least 2.5 million wells have been drilled, with an average of 2.5 wells per square mile in Texas and 4.5 in Oklahoma.

One big, relatively underexplored area is the land belonging to the federal government. It amounts to one-third of the land area of the U.S., mostly in western states and Alaska. In addition, federally controlled offshore (continental shelf) areas are almost as large as the onshore holdings. As of 1980 the U.S. Geological Survey guessed that federally controlled areas contained 37% of the country's undiscovered oil, almost all offshore, and 43% of the undiscovered natural gas, half of it offshore.

The federal share of coal reserves is similar—about 40% lie on public lands. Most eastern coal is privately owned, but in the west the API claims the federal government owns 60% of the coal and controls access to another 20% due to the checkerboard pattern of land ownership. A ten-year moratorium on leasing of federal coal lands, brought on by environmental lawsuits, was only lifted in January 1981 (by the outgoing Carter administration), resulting in a new land rush in the '80s. The energy industry's hopes for expansion center on western coal because more of it can be strip-mined—a faster, cheaper method than underground mining—and because the United Mine Workers are weaker in the west.

Thus in oil, gas and coal the federal government controls a lot of what's left in the ground. So if they're going to free you from oil imports, the energy companies are also going to free you from a lot of those federal lands.

Despite the reluctance taxpayers may feel on turning national parks, prairies, forests and coastal waters over to Exxon and friends, the API assures us that wild animals like oil companies:

> Caribou, moose and their calves can be seen
> grazing within a few hundred yards of drilling

rigs, or resting and browsing beneath the elevated portions of the trans-Alaska pipeline, because it is warmer there and the grass is literally greener.

If you like moose under the pipeline, you'll love strip-mining: "In many instances, reclamation has improved the quality of the land after it has been surface-mined." The oilmen's enthusiasm is not shared by many residents of Appalachian areas that have been stripped:

> In Central Appalachia itself, an estimated 600,000 acres of strip-mined land has been left unreclaimed. . . The strip-miner literally blasts away the sides or top of a mountain. Debris is bulldozed over the side, and the exposed coal is shoveled out. While the process is fast and highly profitable, it leaves the mountain a gaping sore; ecological cycles are upset; timber may take several hundred years to recover; streams and wells are contaminated. Reclamation is expensive and rarely carried out. It is, as some have put it, "like putting lipstick on a corpse."[12]

The underlying problem is the same in Western strip-mining: the faster the coal is ripped out of the ground, the smaller the effort spent on reclamation afterwards, the greater the profits will be. Most of the specific hazards are different, though, in the arid plains where Western coal is found.

There is less chance in the West for small strip-mining operations that escape public notice; almost all the region's coal comes from a few dozen giant mines, making it in principle easier to regulate. However, some Western coal areas, including at least a few that are being mined, are simply too dry to be reclaimed at all. Erosion is likely to turn strip-mine refuse into desolate badlands. The heavily mined Four Corners area (near the intersection of Arizona, New Mexico, Colorado and Utah) may be an unfortunate example.

Even in potentially reclaimable areas, cheap or careless stripping can easily cause irreversible destruction of topsoil or pollution of the underground water table, ruining the land for agriculture. Scarce water supplies are already the focus of intense political conflict in much of the West; one study found that in many Western coal deposits,

> It is by no means certain, however, that the hydrologic (water-bearing) functions can be maintained during mining. Until reliable methods of doing so are devised, surface mining will inevitably endanger the long-term productivity of an area for a cash crop of coal that can be harvested only once.[13]

While one could dwell further on the dangers involved in energy production on federal lands—offshore drilling accidents, for instance, could wipe out fishing, tourism and recreation in coastal areas—there is another side to the push for deregulation. Not only the extraction of oil, gas, and coal, but also the use of these fuels is hemmed in by government restrictions. The plans of the energy industry for burning fossil fuels run smack into the Clean Air Act and other limits on pollution.

Some corporate spokesmen prefer to rant and rave about pollution control. An official of the National Association of Manufacturers fumes that clean air standards seem designed "for the 90 year old jogger with tuberculosis."[14] But the well-oiled publicity apparatus of the petroleum industry avoids such crudeness. It's just wonderful that we've come so far in cleaning up the environment, gushes the API; in fact, we're doing so well that surely we can afford to be reasonable, to compromise, to balance the goal of further environmental progress against the need for energy development. . . .

For the top target of all this reasonableness, the Clean Air Act, the oilmen support any of a number of intricate amendments—the effect of which would be to allow more air pollution in many areas. Also in need of more creative reinterpretation are the Safe Drinking Water Act, the Endangered Species Act, and many more. According to the API, environmental laws have caused lengthy delays or cancellations of power plants, pipelines, oil terminals, refineries and other projects needed to secure our energy independence.

Not all compromises are reasonable, however; not all cancellations and delays are regrettable. There are three major reasons why the controls on air pollution should be made stronger, despite the limits those controls impose on energy development.

First, and most important, crud in the air makes people sick. Many air pollutants increase the rates of emphysema, bronchitis and other lung diseases. Cancers of the lung and throat are more common in urban, industrial communities than in rural ones; a number of cancers are particularly widespread in areas near petroleum refineries and petrochemical plants.[15] The progress in pollution control during the 1970s only began to alleviate these problems, and there is much more that needs to be done—but the API would have us believe that we have reached such a state of grace that we can now afford some backsliding.

Second, fossil fuel burning causes acid rain. Coal is the worst offender, per unit of energy. Sulfur dioxide and nitrogen oxides, released out of the smokestack when coal is burned, form sulfuric and nitric acids on contact with the moisture in the atmosphere. The result is that highly acidic rain falls on regions downwind from coal-burning areas. Acid rain kills fish and plant life in lakes and streams; since it also falls into metropolitan reservoirs, it corrodes urban water pipes and potentially causes health problems as well. Acid rain is increasing, and has already reached serious levels in the eastern United States and Canada.[16]

Finally, anything increasing the amount of carbon dioxide in the air contributes to the "greenhouse effect." Again, any fossil fuel is part of the problem, but coal is the worst. You have probably experienced a small-scale greenhouse effect. If you leave a car sitting in the sun with the windows rolled up, it gets quite hot inside. Light passes easily through the glass; on striking something inside, like car seats, most of the light is converted into heat, which can't escape through the glass nearly as fast as light comes in. (The same effect makes greenhouses warmer than the outside air.) Carbon dioxide in the atmosphere acts like window glass, letting in light but holding on to heat. Thus a steady increase in fossil fuel burning could heat up the atmosphere, causing massive shifts in climate, perhaps melting the polar ice caps and threatening to flood coastal regions. It is still uncertain how fast this will happen, but it is clear that the level of carbon dioxide in the air is going up.[17]

Refineries and power plants are cheaper to build without pollution controls, just as cars are cheaper to make without safety devices. But in both cases the eventual costs to consumers and to innocent bystanders are much greater than the costs of doing it right in the first place. Also, to cite one of the energy industry's favorite complaints, there is no evidence that pollution controls have made coal-fired power plants uncompetitive. Throughout the 1970s, as tough controls were implemented, the cost of coal-burning plants did, of course, rise. But the cost of the major commercial alternative, nuclear power plants, rose much faster—even before Three Mile Island.[18] In other words, making coal burn cleanly, though expensive, is cheaper than the ever-more-costly quest for a way to make uranium fission safely.

Despite intense corporate opposition, some of the construction delays caused by government regulation have in retrospect been good for energy industry finances. When prices of all forms of energy began to shoot up after the oil crisis of 1973–74, businesses and households moved rapidly and apparently permanently toward energy conservation. On average, the U.S. now uses 18% less energy per dollar of GNP (corrected for inflation) than it did in 1973, and there is plenty of room for even more conservation.[19] This means that there is little or no need for new capacity to generate electricity.

Yet for years after the energy crisis began, electric utilities insisted on failing to notice the shift toward conservation, overestimating the demand for electricity, and consequently trying to build a number of unnecessary, expensive plants. A little more obstructionist regulation could have saved some companies even more, as the unhappy owners of various partially-completed power plants could tell you.

A defender of the industry might object that this is circular reasoning, that energy became so expensive as to make conservation attractive in large part because of government regulation. But if conservation is often cheaper than truly clean, safe energy production, that makes it reasonable, from the point of view of society as a whole, to conserve. Unregulated energy production might look cheaper still, but only because of the failure to count the hidden costs of more destruction of public lands, more lung disease, more acid rain, more danger from the greenhouse effect in the future.

Don't Just Stand There

Auto industry opposition to safety and emission controls, and energy industry plans to exploit public resources and bend anti-pollution laws, are only two examples—though two of the most important—of the corporate stake in Reagan's push for deregulation. Similar stories could be told about the goals and grievances of many other businesses. Regulations whose benefits to society as a whole in health, safety and environmental protection far outweigh their costs can still look like obstacles to be removed from the narrow viewpoint of the corporate boardroom. In some cases companies have opposed regulations which eventually turned out to be good for profits, suggesting that stepping back from the daily sales grind to think about the needs of society is even at times a good business practice.

For the corporate world the risks of regulation stretch far beyond the costs that have already been imposed. There is no obvious stopping point to the regulatory process so long as dangerous pollutants, unsafe products and hazardous work practices continue to exist. A company which has not yet suffered significantly from regulation might quite reasonably fear that the social costs and benefits of its operations will in time come under public scrutiny.

This leads to the ideological threat of regulation, in the eyes of the administration's dedicated free marketeers: it is not the failures of regulation, not the occasional silly rules, that are the problem, but rather the very success of federal agencies in affecting deadly serious issues such as health and environmental protection. Reagan's deregulatory crusade aims at eliminating the abundant evidence that controls on business can be good for society. In the words of Murray Weidenbaum, "Don't just stand there, undo something."

CHAPTER 8

Which Way Out?

*I think a lot of people look at us . . . as being
overly aggressive. I would say that either you
believe in the free enterprise system of this country, or you don't believe in it.*

—Mobil Corporation Chairman Rawleigh
Warner Jr.[1]

Mobil is not the only corporation which looks overly aggressive today. One company after another is enjoying newly
won tax breaks, regulatory rollbacks, and employee concessions on wages and work rules. These corporate conquests rest
in large part on the actions of the Reagan administration. Ronald Reagan's policies amount to an insistence that the crisis of
the U.S. economy can only be solved on terms dictated by big
business. The case against these policies has been made
throughout the earlier chapters; this chapter outlines an alternative strategy, one which puts people before profits while
developing a solution to the long-term economic crisis.

As explained in Chapter 1, the crisis appeared in the 1970s
because the bases of post-World War II expansion eroded.

U.S. international power was set back, militarily in Vietnam and economically in trade with Japan and Europe. The era of cheap oil came to an abrupt end, creating hardships for consumers and for many oil-hungry industries. The boom in automobiles and suburbanization slowed down. Changes in the nature of government intervention in the economy undercut former sources of corporate profits. The result was that growth in GNP per worker all but ceased, and inflation spiralled upward.

Reaganomics offers to restore growth and price stability through militarization of society and impoverishment of the working population. A no-nonsense projection of U.S. power abroad; getting the government out of social services and further into buying high-profit, high-technology hardware; driving down wages, working conditions and taxes; ending "environmental extremism"—all this, the story goes, is supposed to make it attractive for corporations to start investing and growing again. Eventually the prosperity will drip down onto the rest of us, but only if we first let those at the top splash about in it alone for quite a while.

Is there an alternative strategy for solving the crisis? Can the U.S. economy be revived in a way that maintains essential services and orients production to human needs? We have the material and human resources needed to achieve such an alternative; the ideas involved are not hard to describe. But the political obstacles are formidable: it is not an alternative which the likes of Ronald Reagan or Mobil's Rawleigh Warner Jr. will find attractive.

In brief, there are four parts to the alternative to Reaganomics. First, funds should be freed for other uses by cutting the military budget and by restoring some of the taxes formerly levied on corporations and on the rich. Second, there should be a federal program of civilian reindustrialization. Labor and capital formerly employed in military production, or idled by recession, should be put to work developing safe, clean energy sources, reinventing mass transit and rebuilding the inner cities. Third, vital social services should be protected and improved. At the same time, humane methods should be sought for lowering the cost of services: socialized medicine could hold down health care expenses; moves toward full employment would

convert jobless people who receive costly benefits into employed workers who pay taxes, thus sharply reducing the federal deficit. Finally, structural changes in the economy would
be needed to make the alternative policies work. In the crisis
atmosphere of World War II it was taken for granted that rapid
reorientation of the economy required public control of prices
and production; equally drastic departures from business as
usual may be required to solve the present economic crisis in
an equitable manner.

Two limitations of this alternative should be noted. First,
this is not a complete political program for opponents of Ronald Reagan. Many critics of Reaganomics, for instance, will
also have important criticisms of the president's social policies,
which are beyond the scope of this short book. Second, this
is not a blueprint for an ideal economy. Many readers will
doubtless be able to suggest worthwhile economic changes
which are not discussed here. The purpose of this alternative
is a more specific one: to propose a strategy for reversing the
economic devastation wrought by Ronald Reagan, and to offer
a solution to the crisis which brought Reaganomics to power.

1: Finding the Funds

We cannot escape from the tragic arithmetic of the federal
budget. If Reagan's military budget and Reagan's tax cut for
the rich remain in place, there is roughly nothing left for alternatives of any kind. More than cosmetic changes in both
Pentagon spending and the tax laws would be required to finance a different economic program.

In the military arena, the decline of U.S. international
power should be acknowledged as an established, irreversible
feature of the world today. No amount of weaponry will restore
the predominance we had over other countries in the 1950s.
Neither additional missiles pointed at Moscow nor additional
Marines menacing Central America will do the trick. Accepting
this fact, we could (as argued in Chapter 4) reduce Reagan's
military budget by close to $100 billion a year without reducing
our ability to defend ourselves and our allies. The savings could
be even greater if a new round of disarmament negotiations
were to succeed.

The paramount reason for disarmament negotiations, of course, is to avoid blowing up the world, not to patch up the federal budget. But the dividends of peace would include vast sums of money, millions of workers, and large quantities of equipment and materials freed for use in meeting civilian needs.

While simply undoing everything Reagan has done would be an excellent beginning for military policy, the question of tax cuts is more complex. People need periodic tax cuts to compensate for inflation and "bracket creep"; as seen in Chapter 3, even with Reagan's tax cut middle- and upper-middle-income households will probably pay as large a share of their incomes to the IRS in 1984 as they did in 1980. The poor will face a growing income tax burden. Thus it does not appear desirable to try to reverse the bulk of Reagan's individual income tax cuts. In fact, equity would require an even larger tax cut for those on the bottom.

For those on top, however, our president has been generous to a fault. The cuts in rates paid by upper-income taxpayers, the special incentives for various forms of savings, the virtual abolition of the estate and gift taxes—these measures are neither fair nor effective in stimulating economic growth. Likewise, the bountiful tax breaks for corporations—the ridiculously rapid depreciation schedules, the boost in the investment tax credit, the new rip-off in tax deductions on leased equipment—have utterly failed to produce the promised supply-side miracles. Reimposing past levels of taxation on corporations and on the rich, and closing some of the tax loopholes that existed before the Reagan administration, would increase federal revenues. This, along with abolition of as much as possible of the military budget, would finance other parts of the alternative to Reaganomics.

2: Civilian Reindustrialization

With many auto, steel and other plants shut down by recession and competition from imports, with weapons factories that will close if we succeed in disarming, industrial policy is a key question for an alternative to Reaganomics. Many of the specific products on which U.S. industry once thrived are likely gone forever: it does not make sense to expect the return of two-ton cars and eight-cylinder engines. But this is not to say that manufacturing in general is becoming obsolete. We will still need to mass-produce plenty of hard physical objects in the future.

The problem is that they will in many cases be quite different objects than we have produced in the past. The goal of government policy should be to move labor and capital as quickly and painlessly as possible into the new industries of the future. Three of the most important areas, in which the federal government should be spending money to expand production, are conservation and clean energy development; public transportation; and inner-city reconstruction. These are the industries that should replace cheap oil, automobiles and suburbanization as the bases of U.S. economic growth.

In energy, heavy use of any fossil fuel involves stiff economic and environmental costs. Most of those costs are steadily rising, as easy-to-get supplies are used up. The major commercial alternative, nuclear power, is proving itself unsafe at any price, with ever-more-expensive precautions failing to resolve either the safety or the waste disposal problems. The Reagan administration asserts that we cannot afford to worry about the environmental, safety and health hazards created by the energy industry; hold your breath as we free ourselves from imported oil and get the economy growing again.

The better alternative would be to stick with the tough regulations, often to make them tougher, even though this is sure to drive up the prices of coal, oil, gas and nuclear power. The regulations are well worth the price: in exchange for higher energy bills now we will be enjoying better health (and lower medical expenses) in years to come; we will be preserving large areas of the country for agricultural, recreational or residential uses in the future, rather than letting them be ravaged today.

Strict environmental protection makes clean alternatives such as conservation and solar power more attractive. Alternative energy efforts began to prosper in the late 1970s, spurred both by high fuel prices and by the Carter administration's modest programs in the area. Much more could be done. For example, if the federal government really wanted to reduce the country's dependence on imported oil, one of the most cost-effective approaches (i.e., saving the most oil per dollar) would be to weatherize low-income housing in northern cities.

In solar energy, photovoltaic cells which produce electricity directly from sunlight are not far from being a viable private industry. Federal purchases of photovoltaics could provide the necessary push into large-scale, low-cost production, just as Pentagon purchases of computer chips did in the past. For industrial energy users, cogeneration—producing heat and electricity at the same time—could often get much more out of present levels of fossil fuel consumption. These and other energy alternatives, while involving some health hazards of their own, are much cleaner than continuing reliance on greater and greater fossil fuel production and use.[2]

Not only the high price of energy, but also the rapid changes in the price, have caused economic problems—as the plight of the auto industry demonstrates. Within less than ten years the price of gasoline has taken four dramatic swings, two ups and two downs. Gas prices of course skyrocketed during the two oil crises, in 1973–74 and 1979–80. In the aftermath of each crisis, 1975–78 and 1981–82, the price of gas rose more slowly than other prices, or even fell. Each time, consumer preferences about the size of cars have promptly responded. Small cars are in demand during and right after an oil crisis; then when prices at the gas pump lag behind the general increases in the cost of living, making gasoline look like a bargain again, car buyers bounce back to the bigger models. As described in Chapter 6, the switch back to big cars was quite pronounced in 1975–78. It was showing up again by early 1982: amid the overall depression of the auto industry, the models that were selling best were once again the big ones.

In the past, U.S. automakers were slow to respond to consumer interest in small cars, and lost considerable ground to imports for that reason. By now, however, the entire industry is painfully aware of the importance of making sizes of cars that consumers will actually buy. The problem is that it is very expensive to convert auto plants from small to big car production, or vice versa. According to UAW estimates, it costs nearly half as much as building the entire plant from the ground up.[3] If energy prices could be held relatively stable for, say, eight years, the cost of conversion could be spread over eight years' worth of cars. If size preferences continue to flip-flop every two years, the cost of converting the plants can be spread only over two years' cars. This makes the cost per car higher, drives up the sticker price and depresses auto sales.

Thus the auto industry has been suffering whiplash injuries from overly rapid swings in the price of gas. Similar problems undoubtedly plague other heavily energy-dependent industries. There appears to be a compelling national interest in preventing such rapid reversals in major prices. In the case of autos, this means higher gasoline taxes during the price slumps to keep consumers and industry focused on the desirability of smaller cars.[4]

In the long run, the price of fossil fuels is sure to continue to rise, making the most energy-intensive industries obsolete. Government policy should not attempt to protect activities which are no longer viable at today's prices; rather, the goal should be to move labor and capital into new, growing fields. For example, the energy path advocated here would require expansion of the conservation, solar and other alternative energy industries, involving extensive construction, rehabilitation and insulation of buildings, manufacture and installation of solar energy equipment, production of cogenerators and the like.

More than the size of our cars has been called into question by the energy crisis. The whole way of life embodied in the suburban sprawl, the idea of living thirty miles from work and ten miles from the supermarket, seems far less sensible than it once did. Use of public transportation has been heading up since 1973, and central cities are once again becoming desirable locations. Unfortunately this recent reversal of priorities confronts the wreckage left behind when the federal government built the freeways and the middle class took to the suburbs: decaying transit systems offering lousy service; deteriorating housing; public schools that are being abandoned by everyone who can afford to; and all the other signs of urban decay.

Reaganomics offers only more of the same decline, cutting funds for mass transit, housing, education and other essential services. An alternative economic strategy would call for investment in mass transit and inner-city reconstruction. Much of the money now squandered on titanium airplanes, nuclear aircraft carriers and tax loopholes should instead be poured into the concrete, the steel and the human services required for urban life.

Mass transit offers substantial energy savings over private automobiles, as well as easing urban congestion and air pollution. A government concerned about solving the energy crisis would be repairing, not continuing to destroy, metropolitan transit systems. For most areas this would mean better bus service. The cost of rail transit, for maintaining tracks, stations and trains, is so high (both in dollars and in energy) that it only makes sense in the most densely populated areas where it can be most heavily used. However, in those densest areas—in downtown New York, Chicago, Philadelphia, Boston and other older cities—life would be unimaginable without the existing subways and trolleys, most of which are badly in need of repair after decades of neglect. Maintenance and upgrading of most existing rail transit, and increased production of buses for lower-density areas, are key parts of an alternative economic strategy.

Similar reorganization is on the agenda for intercity transportation. Passenger airlines, the favored, deluxe mode of travel in the past, are now close to bankruptcy because rising fuel costs and other difficulties (see Chapter 6) are pricing them out of reach of most customers. Airlines are a prime example of an energy-wasting industry which should play a reduced role in the future; the use of airplanes for trips of a few hundred miles should be replaced by improved ground transportation.

On the ground, intercity travel now occurs almost exclusively by automobile. Here, too, public transportation should be expanded; here, too, buses rather than railroads will often be appropriate in view of the low population density of much of the country. Passenger railroads will remain essential from Boston to Washington and in other heavily travelled corridors, but will never be as important to the United States as they are to the more densely populated countries of Europe and Japan.

Within the cities, one of the most crying needs is for rehabilitation or replacement of run-down housing. The only form of housing improvement the private market seems capable of today is conversion of apartments into luxury condominiums. To create or improve low- and middle-income housing, government assistance will be required. At the risk of sounding repetitive, programs slashed under Reagan should be expanded instead.

Even government-aided housing construction depends on the cost and availability of mortgages. Federal programs cannot pay the entire cost of construction themselves (or if they did, they would get very few housing units for their money). Therefore, the government's use of sky-high interest rates as a weapon against inflation will undermine any attempt to revive the construction industry. Wild swings in interest rates cause economic "whiplash injuries" to construction, just as gas prices do to automakers. In construction the damage does not involve expensive retooling for different products, but rather turning all production on and off too quickly. In good years new firms start up and shortages of skilled labor appear; in bad years the smaller firms are bankrupted and skilled workers are idled, perhaps driven into other occupations altogether. Potential advances such as low-cost prefabricated housing can scarcely get off the ground in the face of such erratic sales. Just as rational planning for automobiles requires stable energy prices, rational planning for housing requires stable interest rates (and hence another approach to controlling inflation, about which more below).

The needs of the cities do not end with housing. The flight of the middle class and of urban business has left the older cities with a declining tax base, unable to afford to keep up basic services. Better educational, medical and recreational facilities; repairs to streets, water and sewer systems; restoration of the countless social programs, like rat control, that are being gutted under the current regime—surely these are as worthy of federal generosity as tanks that break down every 43 miles, or amphibious personnel carriers that sink.

In urban reconstruction, as in public transportation and in clean energy development, there are plenty of tasks that need doing, plenty of jobs that need manufacturing, construction and transportation workers to fill them. Civilian reindustrialization along these lines would use our resources and skills to meet our needs. What is lacking is only the political will and power to make this program a reality.

3: Government With a Human Face

The emphasis on reindustrialization is not meant to compete with adequate social services. There can be no question of abandoning those in need. Feeding the hungry, caring for the sick and disabled, providing education and recreation for the young, dignity and security for the old: these are the very purpose of economic activity, the mark that sets human society apart from the jungle, not some minor policy option that can be tossed aside because we're into tanks and tax cuts this year. It is easy to demonstrate what an inefficient, muddleheaded job federal bureaucracies have often done in meeting human needs. But it was not the underlying attempt to meet those needs that was at fault.

Having said that (who would have dreamed, before Reagan, that it could sound so controversial?), it is clear that our alternative is fast becoming expensive. The Pentagon's budget plus the revenue from tax reform might not be enough to pay for both civilian reindustrialization and the restoration of social services. Saving money in the delivery of services is of course the favorite indoor sport of the Reagan administration; it will be incumbent on those who advocate an alternative to see whether the game can be played by different, more progressive rules. There is no room for significant savings in Social Security; however, Medicare and Medicaid costs could be reduced by introduction of a national health care system, and many other social service costs would be lowered by moves toward full employment.

Social Security, the biggest, most expensive civilian program, is facing a short-run budget squeeze. It should be gotten through its immediate problems by allowing the three trust funds to borrow from each other (as was done on a one-time basis for 1982), and, if necessary, by small allocations of other federal revenues. It is ridiculous to make sweeping changes in a very successful program under the gun of a temporary crisis.

Once Social Security survives the mid-1980s, there will be roughly 25 easy years before the real crunch begins. After the year 2010 or so, the elderly proportion of the population will rise sharply; either we will force our senior citizens to live a much meaner existence than before, or we will have to spend much more on Social Security.

Those 25 easy years should be used to phase in new approaches to financing retirement benefits, freeing the system from its dependence on a regressive payroll tax. The far more generous, separate programs for federal civilian and military employee pensions, which together cost the taxpayers more than one-fifth as much as Social Security, should gradually be merged with Social Security itself.[5]

Ultimately, however, additional funds will have to be devoted to retirement. As shown in Chapter 5, the twenty-first century crisis in Social Security will not result from an absolute growth in the number of dependents per worker, but rather from a shift from young to old dependents. The orderly transfer of some of the resources formerly spent on education and child-rearing into support for senior citizens should be a focus of national debate and planning over the next quarter-century.

The high cost of health care is a natural place to look for savings. Medicare, Medicaid and other health programs are absorbing ten cents of every dollar the federal government spends, and this proportion will rise in the future as the elderly population increases. The Reagan response is to cut benefits and raise fees, making medical care a little bit harder to afford each time around.

A better alternative would be to follow the lead of most industrial countries and institute a nationalized health care system. With doctors and hospital staffs working under public control, with drug and medical supply companies closely regulated or nationalized, costs could finally be brought down. Doctors' salaries, while still amply above average to compensate for their years of training, would be well below the levels made possible by today's extortionary fee schedules. Straight salaries instead of fee-for-service payments would eliminate the present economic incentive for doctors and hospitals to order needlessly complex tests and equipment.

Financially speaking, we are already two-fifths of the way to nationalized health care: government agencies pay 40% of all medical expenses. The government and private insurance companies together foot two-thirds of the bill.[6] Thus a public takeover of private health insurance plans, and the payments now going into them, would bring most of the nation's medical expenditures under one roof. It would then be possible for the government to establish a unified system of free or nominal-

fee health care for all, eliminating layer upon layer of paperwork and bureaucracy currently required to prove a patient is
financially eligible to be healed.

The notion that such changes would lead to big savings is
not a guess about an untried utopia. Nationalized health systems exist in Canada and throughout Europe, with impressive
results. The same union medical benefits cost about half as
much to provide in Canada as in the U.S. Several European
countries have lower infant mortality and longer life expectancy
than we do, while spending smaller fractions of their national
incomes on health care.[7]

Even at the present level of 40% public financing of medical care, measures that improve public health will in the long
run save the government money. Tough environmental regulations and pollution controls will make people healthier in the
future—and, therefore, will hold down Medicare and Medicaid
costs. The same logic calls for an end to all government supports to tobacco growers, and for vigorous public campaigns
against smoking: fewer smokers today means fewer cases of
lung cancer, emphysema and other diseases twenty years from
now, an obviously desirable result in itself and a savings in
future health care costs to boot.

The best way to cut costs of many other social programs
is to create jobs. Only poor or unemployed people are eligible
for food stamps, welfare, unemployment compensation, housing subsidies and so on. As people get jobs, or move up from
poverty-level to better-paying employment, they stop receiving
benefits and start paying taxes, decreasing the federal deficit.
Thus job creation programs are often a bargain for taxpayers,
if the reductions in the costs of other programs and the increase
in tax payments are counted. The strategy of putting people
to work in civilian reindustrialization—in clean energy development, public transportation and urban reconstruction—
would not only provide socially useful products, but would
lower social service costs and reduce the deficit as well.

The costs of social services related to unemployment shoot
up when companies shut down. In growing numbers of factory
closings the workers involved are attempting to buy the plant
and run it themselves, often failing for lack of modest (by
corporate standards) sums of money. Economists Barry Blue-

stone and Bennett Harrison have suggested that in many such instances it would be cheaper for the government to help the workers buy the plant and keep it open. That way the factory, and the workers, would continue paying taxes, and the jobless benefits caused by a shutdown would be saved. In some (certainly not all) cases, this radical departure would accomplish Ronald Reagan's objective of holding down social welfare spending and putting people back to work.[8]

More than individual plants are being shut down in the economic slump of the early 1980s. Entire regions dependent on auto, steel, construction and related industries are faced with corporate abandonment. Companies in the same areas have often developed complementary lines of business, supplying and buying from each other in ways that create an industrial complex stronger and more valuable than the sum of its parts. Analyzing one of the most important, and most depressed cases, Dan Luria and Jack Russell argue that Detroit's auto plants, parts suppliers, machine shops, etc., collectively possess a unique "metal-bending" capability. The linkages among local firms ("external economies," in the language of economists) have a value to society that does not show up on any corporate balance sheet. Detroit's metal-bending complex could be put to many socially desirable uses, but no private company will find it profitable to take the lead in the process. Luria and Russell advocate public investment in starting a Detroit energy hardware industry, making things like drills, pumps and cogenerators. Their proposal, in other words, fits well with the approach to reindustrialization outlined above. (They reject another obvious product for Detroit, mass transit vehicles, only out of despair at support for public transportation.)[9]

Similar plans will make sense for many of America's Detroits, recycling older industries into the new tasks of the 1980s and beyond, while also boosting employment and saving money on social services related to joblessness. Moving labor and capital into new activities is the only viable solution for those industries, like autos, which are battered by foreign competition. Big business and the Reagan administration propose to drive wages down far enough to make U.S. industry competitive again—from the workers' standpoint, a painful price to pay even if successful. Another major option, erecting trade barriers to protect U.S. industries, would shelter inefficient, high-priced producers, making consumers pay more for formerly imported goods. It would also run the risk of provoking retaliatory trade barriers in other countries, potentially escalating into a full-fledged trade war in which nobody would win.

Reorienting the economy to meet social needs would reduce the role of internationally traded manufactured goods, and hence lessen the threat of layoffs caused by imports. The alternative economic strategy described here would emphasize construction work and social services, both intrinsically local activities which cannot be imported. Manufacturing of products that compete with imports would not be eliminated, but would account for a smaller fraction of the labor force and of national income than in the past.

A full employment policy, putting people to work meeting the needs of the future, is the most important part of the answer to joblessness and welfare-related costs. But it is not by itself sufficient. As some companies close (not all will be worth saving, by any criterion) and others open, as technologies and job requirements seem to change more rapidly than before, many people will find the skills and experience they have acquired becoming obsolete long before their work lives are over. Even if there are enough openings to go around, nothing automatically fits old workers into new jobs. Moreover, some groups face other obstacles to employment. Most welfare recipients are single mothers who cannot take jobs unless child care is available as well. (Some would choose to stay home with their children in any case, and should be allowed to; many would choose to work if it were possible, thereby creating big reductions in welfare costs.)

A humane welfare policy, therefore, would emphasize services such as job retraining programs and expansion of child care. The objective is, in a sense, the same as that of the Reagan administration: to get people off welfare and other benefits, and into paid work. The difference is that one approach makes it increasingly possible for people to leave welfare, by providing them with the skills and support necessary to earn a better living; the other approach makes it increasingly impossible for people to remain on welfare, through regulations that harass and disqualify many who are still in need.

4: Controlling Prices and Production

More than a few times, the alternative economic strategy presented here calls for expanding programs that Reagan has slashed, for undoing the damage that Reaganomics has done. The question is bound to arise, therefore: in what ways is this different from the old liberalism which failed in the 1970s?

The answer is in part a matter of degree. Both throwing pebbles into the waves and flying across the ocean involve airborne motion in the same direction, though with rather different results. Jimmy Carter never confessed in public to any serious interest in cutting half or more of the military budget, ending dependence on fossil fuels and nuclear power, or socializing health care. At best one might view his position, and the liberalism of the mainstream of the Democratic Party in general, as including occasional friendly nods towards some of the pieces of an alternative economic strategy—pleasanter than Ronald Reagan, to be sure, but falling far short of actually reorganizing production to meet human needs.

At a certain point a successful alternative to Reaganomics would have to depart from traditional liberalism in direction as well as in degree. The parting of the ways comes when the going gets rough, when it comes time to fight inflation. Both Democratic and Republican administrations have remained trapped within the logic of the inflation/unemployment trade-off, unable to control prices except by throwing millions of people out of work every few years. The commitment to creating jobs and getting people back to work evaporates as soon as inflation reappears; instead, budget cuts and high interest rates are used to create another recession and another brief episode of slower price hikes.

This trade-off is no accident; it is a result of the rules of the capitalist system. As long as workers and employers must struggle to defend their own incomes and as long as that struggle is what determines wages and prices, then full employment will lead to inflation. Workers will find that times of full employment offer the best chances for gains in wages and working conditions; businesses will find that times of high consumer incomes offer the best opportunities for raising prices. In a recession, on the other hand, unemployment weakens the bargaining power of labor, and lower consumer incomes discourage businesses from raising prices quite as fast. As seen in Chapter 1, the trade-off appears to be worsening; more and more unemployment is required to achieve the same amount of reduction in inflation.

It would be nice to announce, as the Reagan administration repeatedly does, that the brilliance of a new policy will abolish the trade-off and allow simultaneous, easy solutions to both inflation and unemployment.[10] But in truth, it would be no more realistic for our alternatives than for theirs. There are only three choices: to live with inflation, probably ever-worsening inflation, as a result of full employment; to live with periodic recessions, probably ever-worsening recessions, as the means of limiting inflation; or to change the rules of the free market, to create direct controls on prices. In other words, the only route to full employment and price stability is through controls. Without controls, there is no real hope of maintaining full employment in the face of spiralling prices.

Price controls are not a simple solution. They tend to become unworkable because of the way they interfere with the market. Freely changing prices, much as they are disliked by consumers, do play an important role in directing production. In a capitalist economy, even a monopolized one, price fluctuations are the signals which guide the decisions of businesses and individuals. If a commodity becomes scarce, its price will rise, inducing more production of the item; if this is not allowed to happen, a shortage could develop.

There are always some big questions on which the government steps in and alters the signals sent by the market. Reaganomics makes a set of political choices about funding for weapons vs. housing, for airlines vs. mass transit, for nuclear vs. solar energy; our alternative would make the opposite choices. Lurking below the level of big, explicit political choices, however, are the countless mini-decisions: how much of society's resources should be allocated to producing tomatoes vs. lettuce, or pants vs. shirts, or steel sheets vs. steel pipes? The signals of price fluctuations are not the ideal mechanism for allocating resources, but they are the way the U.S. economy works. Eliminating this mechanism without providing a substitute is asking for trouble—specifically, asking for shortages to appear.

This argument needs to be taken seriously, but does not completely outweigh the opposing reasons for controls. Workers and consumers need a way to achieve relief from inflation without repeated bouts of nine or ten percent unemployment. Even businesses suffer when prices move too far and too fast, as in the whiplash effect of gas prices on the auto industry or of interest rates on construction. While businesses want the freedom to respond to small price changes, they too need protection from big, abrupt changes in costs if they are to carry out rational planning for investment and production.*

Some—certainly not all—of the problems with controls might be avoided by allowing small price fluctuations, while prohibiting the biggest, fastest jumps. The mass media have focused on "double-digit" increases as the level at which inflation becomes truly painful. So suppose that all prices, wages of all but the lowest-paid workers, and interest rates were prevented from rising by more than 10% per year. It is possible that such a formula would leave room for price fluctuations to carry out much of their appointed role, while also blocking the worst effects of inflation. If it worked smoothly, the ceiling could be lowered below 10% in later years.

Anti-inflation tax incentives, suggested by some liberal economists, might be another route to the same goal of "loose"

---

*A theoretical digression: why doesn't the market allocate resources efficiently in the face of frequent, drastic price swings? Textbook analysis typically examines the response to a single change in prices, thereby implicitly assuming the new prices will continue indefinitely—or at least long enough for investments made in response to the new prices to pay for themselves. In the past this assumption did not seem unrealistic. Today, one of the manifestations of economic crisis is the threat of overly frequent price changes. If producers expect that the prices which motivate their investments may not last long, they will demand exorbitant prices and profit rates in order to recover the cost of the investments quickly; their high prices will depress production in general. Only in the most pedantically abstract sense could this outcome be called "efficient."

price control. Tax breaks could be used to reward those who
have below-average price and wage increases, while higher
taxes could penalize above-average increases. This, too, would
have its problems: tax incentives often turn out to be expensive,
inefficient means of achieving social goals. Still, it is an approach which deserves consideration.

If some system of price control is enacted, the economy,
freed of the need for frequent recessions, could remain much
closer to full employment. Formerly unemployed workers
would gain the self-respect and security, as well as the incomes,
that accompany steady jobs; production would increase; social
welfare spending and government deficits would be reduced.
High interest rates would no longer be needed to slow down
the economy and control inflation; lower interest rates would
boost construction and other activities dependent on borrowing. The advantages of finding some way to stop inflation without recessions make it well worth the experimentation and
trouble which it is sure to involve.

Just as a program of full employment leads to the need
for price controls, the attempt to make price controls work
leads on to the need for social regulation of production. Capitalists can always go on strike against price controls, refusing
to expand production at controlled prices and thus allowing
shortages to develop. Sudden scarcities of an essential product
like gasoline, as the oil companies have been kind enough to
demonstrate twice so far, create an atmosphere of panic in
which price hikes and other corporate goals can be achieved
with ease. Capital strikes have proved much more reliably successful than their labor counterparts.

Any strategy that conflicts with the corporate agenda must
be prepared for this scenario: controls or other interference
with business as usual can lead to shortages. It is not an in-
surmountable obstacle; it was overcome during our most successful past episode of price controls, in World War II. Those
controls, like any others, created continual tendencies toward
shortages.

The wartime air of urgency and common purpose allowed
many unconventional economic measures. Direct government
regulation of war-related production overcame many short-

ages; rationing and voluntary conservation to aid the war effort coped with other scarcities. In many cases where existing industrial capacity to produce war materials was inadequate, the government stepped in and invested in new plants and equipment. By 1945 the federal Defense Plant Corporation had financed more than 2,000 industrial facilities, and owned more than 900 of them. Other government agencies provided additional aid to boost production of synthetic rubber and strategic materials.[11]

When there was a war to be won, no one waited around for private enterprise to perform. It was not necessary to use higher prices to bribe the economy into higher output. Could it be that our war planners found public enterprise a faster, more efficient way to get the job done? The evidence for this subversive conclusion was hastily disposed of after the war, as the publicly owned industrial plants were soon sold to private corporations at bargain prices.

In peacetime, less abundant but still unmistakeable evidence shows that public ownership is not always the kiss of death to business concerns. The fabled incompetence of Amtrak and the Postal Service is not an inevitable feature of government enterprises, as two major, well-known cases demonstrate. Renault, the French auto company, was nationalized just after World War II. It has thrived under public control, managing—unlike some of America's leading capitalists—to produce the right car at the right time throughout the 1970s. By 1980 it was selling more cars in Europe than any other company.[13] Back in the U.S., the Tennessee Valley Authority has provided low-cost power to a large area of the country since the 1930s, rivalling any privately owned utility in efficiency. Neither one is a utopia: Renault treats its workers no better than similar private firms do, and the TVA is as insensitive to environmental concerns as any other utility. But neither one is the catastrophe conjured up by the mythology of public ineptitude.

As long as the government *can* run large enterprises efficiently, perhaps it should do so more often. If private companies refuse to produce essential goods and services at stable prices, the government should instead. This is one of the arguments for a national health care system: medical care is widely viewed as a human right to which everyone is entitled, in which withholding services from those unable to pay is morally unacceptable. Only public control of health care can guarantee access for all at controlled prices; private enterprise will never do it.

The argument is just as true for other necessities such as energy. None of us chose to live in a world in which gasoline is essential to almost everyone's daily life. But since we do, it is outrageous to let a handful of multinational corporations turn the supplies off every few years in the pursuit of higher profits. At the very least the U.S. should establish a public oil company to exploit the oil on federal lands, and to provide a benchmark against which to judge the prices and performance of private firms. Better yet would be a public takeover of the energy industry as a whole, allowing investment of much of the profits in the development of clean energy alternatives.

Similar arguments could be made about other industries as well. Only if the government is prepared to engage in production of essential goods and services—as it did of war materials in World War II—will it be possible to maintain price controls and reorient production to human needs.

If ideas like these were to take hold, the government would find itself nationalizing a number of existing corporations. One of the factors determining the success or failure of a nationalized enterprise is the price at which the government buys it. Typically the former owners are given government bonds as payment, and the public enterprise then has to pay interest on the bonds for years to come. If the purchase price is too high, the enterprise is stuck with excessive interest costs from the start, forcing it to charge high prices and making it look inefficient.

Part of the success of Renault is due to the particularly attractive price at which the French government picked it up: zero. The owners had been Nazi collaborators during World War II, and the postwar government therefore seized their assets without compensation. In France, as in the United States, World War II prompted the political mobilization necessary to make government intervention in production a success. Can it be done without a war?

The sketch of an alternative to Reaganomics is now complete. It begins by slashing the military budget and reimposing the taxes once paid by corporations and by the rich; it continues with a program of civilian reindustrialization, moving labor and capital into clean energy development, mass transit and urban reconstruction. It maintains adequate human services, including gradual reform of Social Security financing, socialization of health care, and commitment to full employment—both as an end in itself and as a means of reducing social welfare costs. Finally, the alternative calls for price controls as the only way to reconcile full employment and price stability; and it requires public production of necessary goods and services at controlled prices whenever private enterprise refuses to do so. This is an alternative which takes us far from the familiar contours of the U.S. economy, far along the path to what many would call socialism—but it is the only route to an economy that works for most of us.

After Reaganomics

> My own country learns nothing except by dreadful experience.
>
> —John Maynard Keynes, 1940.[13]

Keynes' lament for Britain in 1940 is no less true of the U.S. in the 1980s. Only the dreadful experience of seeing Ronald Reagan in power could convince a majority of our country of the hollowness, the deceit, the hidden agenda behind his well-rehearsed pitch. Let us hope the lesson has now been learned. No, slashing away the civilian functions of government does not create freedom, opportunity and soaring incomes, except for those who were already on top. No, bringing the world to the brink of war does not restore our long-departed global supremacy. Strip-mining the land and fouling the air is not the answer to the energy crisis; senior citizens receiving Social Security are not the cause of inflation; and on and on.

As this book goes to press, ten million people want to work but cannot because of Reaganomics. Try to picture the work of ten million pairs of hands not being done: the metal and wood not shaped, the clothes not sewn, the trucks not driven, the teaching, healing, caring for those in need that is not taking place. There are more than enough tasks crying to be done; it is not hard to describe an alternative strategy for reviving the economy and putting people back to work, for reorienting production to meet social needs.

The obstacles to such an alternative are above all political. It is not in the interests of big business to see the country move in this direction. Indeed, our alternative calls for tighter controls and regulation of corporations, even nationalization of recalcitrant cases. This alternative will not be granted to us from above. The conservatives entrenched in power are of course opposed, and the surviving congressional liberals have largely failed to take the initiative in countering Reagan's policies.

It is only through grassroots political action that there is any hope of reversing the tide of Reaganomics. When unions, community groups, women's and minority organizations, and new coalitions are heard demanding change, when members of Congress are inundated by angry voters telling them to stand up to the president, there will be a chance to undo what Ronald Reagan has done. The recent upsurge of anti-war activity, opposing both the nuclear arms race and intervention in Central America, is a promising example of resistance; so, too, are the quietly effective senior lobbies which have defended Social Security and Medicare, and the tenacious environmental organizations which have blocked some of the worst schemes hatched by James Watt. The future of our society, perhaps of the world, rests on the success of the opposition to the Reagan administration.

In early 1982 a Republican congressman from Pennsylvania, Marc Lincoln Marks, declared that he would not be running for re-election, and felt suddenly free to speak his mind about the policies of his party. One can hardly do better in closing than to quote his words. "The time has come to stop this massacre!" he said. He proceeded to blast "a President and his cronies, whose belief in Hooverism has blinded them to the wretchedness and the suffering they are inflicting" on anyone "other than those fortunate enough to insulate themselves in a corporate suit of armor." The congressman went on to urge the country to action:

The time is now, to call out to thinking men and women everywhere to raise their voice against this murderous mandate . . . .[14]

FOOTNOTES TO CHAPTER 1

1. This article is also the source of all later Stockman quotes unless otherwise noted. The passage quoted here reflects Stockman's thinking around the time of the 1980 election.
2. On patterns of U.S. foreign investment, see "Stalking Profits Overseas," *Dollars & Sense,* December 1981.
3. U.S. Department of Commerce, Bureau of the Census, *Statistical Abstract of the United States, 1980,* p. 648, and *Historical Statistics of the United States, Colonial Times to 1970,* p. 716. These Census volumes are basic sources for many of the statistics used in this book; hereafter they will be cited as *1980 Statistical Abstract* and *Historical Statistics.* When no source is cited for a statistic in the text, it may be assumed to come from the appropriate table in these works or in *Economic Report of the President, January 1981.*
4. *Historical Statistics,* p. 620.
5. The account of the size and composition of government spending in this chapter is largely based on "Big Government, Big Taxes," *Dollars & Sense,* July–August 1981, and on James T. Campen and Arthur MacEwan, "Crisis, Contradictions and Conservative Controversies in Contemporary U.S. Capitalism," (unpublished; University of Massachusetts/Boston, 1981), p. 14–18.
6. See Campen and MacEwan, *op. cit.,* p. 15.
7. These are December to December increases in the consumer price index.
8. *Boston Globe,* February 3, 1982.

FOOTNOTES TO CHAPTER 2

1. Milton and Rose Friedman, *Free to Choose* (New York: Harcourt Brace Jovanovich, 1980), p. 141.
2. *Ibid.,* p. 215.
3. *Ibid.,* p. 223.
4. *Ibid.,* p. 106.
5. *Ibid.,* p. 137.
6. *Ibid.,* p. 13.
7. George Gilder, *Wealth and Poverty,* (New York: Basic Books, 1981), p. 258.
8. *Ibid.,* p. 77.
9. *Ibid.,* p. 99–100.
10. *Ibid.,* p. 28, p. 50.
11. *Ibid.,* p. 69.
12. *Ibid.,* p. 114–115.
13. See the Census Bureau's *1980 Statistical Abstract,* p. 354.
14. Gilder, p. 14.
15. *Ibid.,* p. 135, p. 131.
16. *Ibid.,* p. 138–139.
17. *Ibid.,* p. 51–52.
18. *Ibid.,* p. 24–27.
19. *Ibid.,* p. 181.
20. *Ibid.,* p. 235.
21. *Ibid.,* p. 262.
22. *Ibid.,* p. 252, p. 263, p. 268.

FOOTNOTES TO CHAPTER 3

1. The evaluation of supply-side effects and references to the economic literature in the rest of this chapter are based on Campen and MacEwan, *op. cit.*, p. 31–45, and on Robert Buchele, "Supply Side Economics Meets the Real World" (Smith College Economics Department, 1981). The estimates of tax losses from the 1981 cuts and the details of the cuts themselves are taken from the "Joint Explanatory Statement" of the Congressional conference committee which produced the final version of the tax act: *House of Representatives Report 97–215*, p. 196–292.
2. The extensive literature on the subject is cited in Campen and MacEwan, *op. cit.*, p. 39-40, and Buchele, p. 6-7.
3. The supply-side study is M.J. Boskin, "Taxation, Saving, and the Rate of Interest," *Journal of Political Economics,* April 1978, Part 2. Criticisms of it are summarized in Campen and MacEwan, *op. cit.*, p. 40-41, and Buchele, *op. cit.*, p. 9-10.
4. Campen and MacEwan, *op. cit.*, p. 42 (footnote) derive this conclusion, even if Boskin's controversial results are accepted.
5. See Buchele, *op. cit.*, p. 10.
6. *Business Week,* November 9, 1981.
7. *New York Times,* January 31, 1982.
8. For an evaluation of the proposed return to the gold standard, see *Dollars & Sense,* November 1981.

FOOTNOTES TO CHAPTER 4

1. As forecast in *America's New Beginning: A Program for Economic Recovery* (White House, February 18, 1981), part III, page 11.
2. Philip Morrison and Paul F. Walker, "A New Strategy for Military Spending", *Scientific American,* October 1978, p. 52.
3. *Ibid.*, p. 53.
4. James Fallows, *National Defense* (New York: Random House, 1981), p. 148-157.
5. *Boston Globe,* January 18, 1982; *Esquire,* March 1982.
6. Morrison and Walker, *op. cit.*, p. 51-52.
7. Arthur Macy Cox, "The CIA and the Soviet Threat," *New York Review of Books,* November 6, 1980; Franklyn Holzman, "Are the Soviets Really Outspending the U.S. on Defense?", *International Security,* Spring 1980; conversation with Franklyn Holzman.
8. This and related statistical biases in the CIA estimates, too numerous and technical to describe here, are explained in Holzman, *op. cit.*, and Holzman, "Soviet Military Spending: Assessing the Numbers Game," *International Security,* Spring 1982.
9. Holzman (1980) *op. cit.*, p. 101 (footnote 35).
10. As cited in David Cortright and Michelle Stone, "Military Budget Manual" (Washington DC.: National SANE Education Fund, 1981), p. 3.
11. Fallows, *op. cit.*, p. 50.
12. *Wall Street Journal,* February 17, 1982.
13. Fallows, *op. cit.*, p. 35-49.
14. *Boston Globe,* February 7, 1982: *New York Times,* February 14, 1982.

15. Boston Study Group, *The Price of Defense* (New York: Times Books, 1979). Morrison and Walker, *op. cit.*, is a useful summary of the book; the quote is from Morrison and Walker, p. 50.

16. *Dollars & Sense,* December 1981.

17. Michael T. Klare, "The Feeble Giant", *The Nation,* October 24, 1981.

18. Morrison and Walker, *op. cit.*, p. 55-57.

19. *Defense Monitor,* September–October 1977.

20. John Maynard Keynes, "The United States and the Keynes Plan," *New Republic,* July 29, 1940. In his far better-known *General Theory of Employment, Interest and Money,* (Chapter 10, Section VI), Keynes suggested that "It would, indeed, be more sensible to build houses and the like," but recognized that "Pyramid-building, earthquakes, even wars may serve to increase wealth, if the education of our statesmen on the principles of the classical economics stands in the way of anything better."

21. *1980 Statistical Abstract,* p. 372–373.

22. On employment from alternative programs, see Michael Edelstein, "The Economic Impact of Military Spending," (New York: Council on Economic Priorities, 1977). On the productivity effect, see, for instance, Seymour Melman, "Looting the Means of Production," *New York Times,* July 26, 1981.

23. Military purchases from corporations were $60.9 billion in fiscal 1979 (*1980 Statistical Abstract,* p. 372; this is the procurement total from table 604, excluding "intragovernmental" and "educational and non-profit institutions" procurement. This was somewhat over 4% of the calendar 1979 gross domestic product of nonfinancial corporations (*1981 Economic Report of the President,* p. 246). Considerable anecdotal evidence suggests that the rate of profit is higher on military contracts than on average corporate sales; making the admittedly arbitrary assumption that the rate of profit as a percentage of sales in military contracting is twice the corporate average, I arrive at my 8% estimate.

24. See, for instance *Economic Report of the President, February 1982,* p. 85–87.

FOOTNOTES TO CHAPTER 5

1. *Boston Globe,* January 18, 1982.

2. *Boston Globe,* February 18, 1982.

3. Hints of a future attack can be found throughout the 1983 budget documents. For instance, "The President seeks to develop a bipartisan consensus to resolve the problems threatening the financial stability of social security. A bipartisan National Commission on Social Security Reform has been established to address these issues and report its recommendations by January 1983." *(Budget of the United States Government, Fiscal Year 1983,* page 5–145). In other words, let's try again just after the Congressional elections . . .

4. *New York Times,* February 7, 1982.

5. This uses the administration's optimistic assumption of 6% inflation (*Fiscal 1983 Budget,* page 2–5). It would be more appropriate to use estimates of the cost in 1983 of maintaining 1982 service levels (and, since the administration also assumes unemployment will be one percentage point lower in

1983, that "current services" cost would be somewhat lower). However, the 1983 budget is organized in a way which makes current service cost comparisons difficult.

6. Unless otherwise noted, the sources for the following descriptions of budget cuts are: for 1983, *Fiscal 1983 Budget* and the summaries of it appearing in the *New York Times* and the *Boston Globe* on February 7, 1982; for 1982, the president's *Program for Economic Recovery* (February 1981) and *Additional Details on Budget Savings* (April 1981), and the summary of the impact of the fiscal 1982 budget found in the *Boston Globe*, January 18, 1982.

7. *Wall Street Journal*, November 20, 1981.

8. *UAW Research Bulletin*, December 1981–January 1982, and conversation with Leon Potok, UAW Research Department.

9. John Steinbeck, *The Grapes of Wrath*, (New York: Bantam Books edition, 1969), p. 384–385.

10. *Boston Globe*, January 18, 1982.

11. *Boston Globe*, February 15, 1982.

12. *Dollars & Sense*, February 1982, based on research by Caroline Chauncey.

13. *Boston Globe*, March 7, 1982.

14. The title of a feature article, *U.S. News & World Report*, September 21, 1981.

15. *Wall Street Journal*, November 20, 1981.

16. *New York Times*, May 10, 1981.

17. *Boston Globe*, February 15, 1982.

18. *New York Times*, December 27, 1981.

19. *Ibid.; Boston Globe*, February 15, 1982.

20. *Boston Globe*, January 18, 1982.

21. *Business Week*, February 8, 1982.

22. *New York Times*, December 6, 1981, based on Census data for 1978.

23. *Business Week*, September 28, 1981.

24. Testimony of Douglas Fraser to the Social Security Subcommittee of the Ways and Means Committee, U.S. House of Representatives, June 10, 1981, p. 2-3.

25. *Business Week*, September 28, 1981.

26. As cited in James H. Schulz, *The Economics of Aging* (Belmont, California: Wadsworth Publishing Company, second edition, 1980), p. 11.

27. Although Table 3 is based on Census Series II-X, the same conclusion can be reached using Series I, II or III. See table sources.

28. The last two assumptions probably lead to an overstatement of the future number of dependents per worker. Immigration is likely to continue, and immigrants include a much higher proportion of working-age people than does the population as a whole. And a higher percentage of the adult population may well work outside the home in the future, since there will be fewer children per adult.

29. If all workers were in the 18–64 age range, then the number of young and old dependents per worker, using the data in Table 3, would be the sum of columns 1 and 2, divided by column 4. This ratio declines from 1.19 in 1960 to 0.99 in the long-run limit. In fact, the vast majority of workers are aged 18 to 64, so these ratios cannot be far off.

30. Schulz, *op. cit.*, p. 54, p. 63.

FOOTNOTES TO CHAPTER 6

1. *Washington Post,* December 17 and 23, 1980; *Business Week,* December 29, 1980.
2. *Wall Street Journal,* February 12, 1981.
3. Interview with Harley Shaiken, *Dollars & Sense,* January 1982; and information supplied by Dan Luria, UAW Research Department.
4. *Business Week,* December 21, 1981.
5. See *Dollars & Sense,* May-June 1979, or *Trade Wars* (Dollars & Sense, 1979).
6. *New York Times,* February 14, 1982.
7. *Ibid.*
8. *Boston Globe,* March 5, 1982.
9. *1980 Statistical Abstract,* p. 428, 430; NEA membership figures supplied by NEA's Massachusetts office.
10. *Dollars & Sense,* January 1982; *New York Times,* December 27, 1981.
11. *Dollars & Sense,* October 1981; Richard W. Hurd, "Inquest on a Strike: How PATCO Was Led Into a Trap," *The Nation,* December 26, 1981. The *Dollars & Sense* coverage of PATCO was also based on Hurd's work.
12. This account of OSHA is adapted from *Dollars & Sense,* October 1981, based largely on the work of Faye Brown.

FOOTNOTES TO CHAPTER 7

1. *New York Times,* November 1, 1981.
2. *New York Times,* January 31, 1982.
3. Murray L. Weidenbaum, "The High Cost of Government Regulation," *Challenge,* November-December 1979.
4. William K. Tabb, "Government Regulations: Two Sides to the Story," *Challenge,* November-December 1980.
5. *Ibid.;* conversation with Carol Pierson, WGBH-FM, Boston.
6. Jewell Westerman, "A Difference of Opinion," *Fortune,* May 4, 1981.
7. Ruth Ruttenberg, "Regulation is the Mother of Invention," *Working Papers,* May-June 1981, and "The Gold in Rules," *Environmental Action,* October 1981; Samuel Epstein, *The Politics of Cancer* (Garden City, New York: Anchor Press, 1979), pp. 103–110.
8. *1980 Statistical Abstract,* p. 217.
9. The interview with Roger Smith appeared in *New York Times,* November 1, 1981.
10. *1980 Statistical Abstract,* p. 216.
11. American Petroleum Institute, *Two Energy Futures,* 1980. This treatment of it is adapted from *Dollars & Sense,* February 1981.
12. John Gaventa, "In Appalachia: Property is Theft," *Southern Exposure,* Volume I Number II (1973).
13. Genevieve Atwood, "The Strip-Mining of Western Coal, *"Scientific American,* December 1975.
14. Gail Robinson, "Gunning for the Clean Air Act," *Environmental Action,* February 1981.
15. Epstein, *op. cit.,* pp. 48–50.
16. Gene E. Likens et al., "Acid Rain," *Scientific American,* October 1979.

17. George M. Woodwell, "The Carbon Dioxide Question," *Scientific American*, January 1978.

18. See the interview with Charles Komanoff, a consultant on power plant economics, in *Dollars & Sense*, March 1980.

19. See the *Dollars & Sense* special issue on the energy crisis, July-August 1980, and also *Dollars & Sense*, May-June 1982.

FOOTNOTES TO CHAPTER 8

1. *New York Times*, December 20, 1981.

2. On the overall economics of alternative energy sources, see *Dollars & Sense*, July-August 1980. On the chemical hazards involved in photovoltaic cell production, see *Dollars & Sense*, December 1980.

3. Information supplied by Dan Luria of the UAW Research Department.

4. This position would even be surprisingly popular with some of the auto companies. By March 1982 Chrysler was advocating a 25-cents-a-gallon tax on gasoline to slow the accelerating switch back to big cars. *New York Times*, March 21, 1982.

5. Military pensions, included in military spending in Table 2 (and in most discussions of the federal budget), accounted for $15 billion of spending in fiscal 1982 and a projected $16 billion for 1983; see *Fiscal Year 1983 Budget*, p. 5–10. Civilian federal employee pensions are shown separately in Table 2.

6. *1980 Statistical Abstract*, p. 104.

7. The lower cost of union benefits in Canada was cited in Chapter 6. On mortality and life expectancy, see *1980 Statistical Abstract*, p. 901–902. On the level of European vs. U.S. health expenditures, see Victor W. Sidel and Ruth Sidel, *A Healthy State: An International Perspective on the Crisis in U.S. Medical Care* (New York: Pantheon, 1977), p. 118–119; J.G. Simanis, "Medical Care Expenditures in Seven Countries," *Social Security Bulletin*, March 1973, p. 39–40.

8. Barry Bluestone and Bennett Harrison, *Capital and Communities: The Causes and Consequences of Private Disinvestment* (Washington, D.C.: Progressive Alliance, 1980).

9. Dan Luria and Jack Russell, *Rational Reindustrialization* (Detroit, 1981).

10. The alleged abolition of the trade-off by Reaganomics is mentioned throughout the president's February 1981 *Program for Economic Recovery*, and again in the *Economic Report of the President, February 1982*, p. 48–52.

11. Martin Carnoy and Derek Shearer, *Economic Democracy* (White Plains, N.Y.: M.E. Sharpe, 1980), p. 63–64.

12. *Fortune*, May 4, 1981; Carnoy and Shearer, *op. cit.*, p. 41–46.

13. John Maynard Keynes, "The United States and the Keynes Plan," *New Republic*, July 29, 1940.

14. *Boston Globe*, March 10, and March 16, 1982.